Knaves, Fools, Madmen, and that Subtile Effluvium

University of Florida Monographs

Social Sciences Number 62

Knaves, Fools, Madmen, and that Subtile Effluvium

A Study of the Opposition to the French Prophets in England, 1706–1710

Hillel Schwartz

A University of Florida Book

The University Presses of Florida
Gainesville / 1978

EDITORIAL COMMITTEE

Social Sciences Monographs

Library of Congress Cataloging in Publication Data

Schwartz, Hillel, 1948–
  Knaves, fools, madmen, and that subtile effluvium.

  (University of Florida monographs: Social
sciences; no. 62)
  "A University of Florida book."
  Bibliography: p.
  Includes index.
  1. Millennialism—England. 2. Millennialism—
France. 3. Huguenots—France. 4. Huguenots—
England. 5. Enthusiasm. 6. England—Church
history—18th century. I. Title. II. Series:
Florida. University, Gainesville. University of
Florida monographs: Social sciences; no. 62.
BR758.S35   272'.4'0941   78–1692
ISBN 0–8130–0505–1

Printed in Florida

The University Presses of Florida is the scholarly
publishing agency for the State University System
of Florida.

Acknowledgments

I WISH to thank Professor David F. Musto, M.D., for his assistance and suggestions. Dr. David Pariente and Michael Donnelly also provided me with insights and strategies of analysis. I am much obliged to Mr. and Mrs. T. Lindsay Stack for their hospitality, help, and permission to cite the manuscripts in their possession. Ms. Irene Scouloudi secured me access to the Archives of the French Protestant Church, Soho Square (London), and M. de Tocqueville kindly granted me permission to consult the Fonds Lamoignon in the Chartrier de Tocqueville at the Archives Nationales (Paris). Mrs. Eva Murray-Browne has similarly granted me permission to cite the Lloyd Papers on microfilm at the Worcestershire Record Office. Professors John Walsh and Margaret C. Jacob have shared with me both conversation and references.

This monograph is an extensive revision of a part of my dissertation, "The French Prophets in England: A Social History of a Millenarian Group in the Early Eighteenth Century" (Yale, 1974). Discussion of the history of the French Prophets has here been severely abbreviated, and much of the necessary background and narrative has been supplied without elaborate documentation. A larger work on the history of the French Prophets is in progress.

Thanks must go also to the Graduate School of the University of Florida for making possible the publication of this monograph.

NOTES AND ABBREVIATIONS

B.P.U.G.   Bibliothèque publique et universitaire de Genève

Fatio Calendar   Nicolas Fatio de Duillier, unfoliated calendar of
                  events in shorthand, 1706–10, in B.P.U.G., MSS
                  fr. 601.

Lacy, *Warnings* John Lacy, *The Prophetical Warnings of John*
I, II, or III   *Lacy, Esq; pronounced under the Operation of the*
                  Spirit, 3 vols., London, 1707, the third volume
                  having a variant title, *Warnings of the Eternal*
                  Spirit by the Mouth of his Servant, John, sir-
                  named Lacy.

Stack MSS   Private manuscript collection of Mr. T. Lindsay
                  Stack, London.

Dates. All dates are in Old Style (O.S.) unless otherwise marked for
the New Style (N.S., Gregorian). The English year began on March
25, Lady Day. English dates between January 1 and March 24 are
traditionally given with both years: January 26, 1707/8.

Quotations. All spellings except those in poetry and in titles of
printed works have been modernized. Italics have been omitted
wherever used simply as standard printer's technique for identifying
proper names or indicating quotations. In the latter case, quotation
marks have been substituted.

Footnoting Procedures. Publication place and date and full title are
provided for all secondary sources in the first reference. Thereafter,
the references have a short title. Full titles for major primary
sources are provided in the Bibliography.

Contents

. . . their Countenance changes, and is no longer Natural; their Eyes roll after a ghastly manner in their Heads, or they stand altogether fixed; all the Members of their Body seem displaced, their Hearts beat with extraordinary Efforts and Agitations; they become Swelled and Bloated, and look bigger than ordinary; they Beat themselves with their Hands with a vast Force, like the miserable Creature in the Gospel, cutting himself with Stones; the Tone of their Voice is stronger than what it could be Naturally; their Words are sometimes broken and interrupted; they speak without knowing what they speak, and without remembering what they have Prophesied.

Marc Vernous, *A Preservative against the False Prophets of the Times* (London, 1708), pp. 23–24.

God deliver us all from Infatuation.

Observator, July 23–26, 1707.

1. Backgrounds

IN THE SUMMER of 1706, three prophets from Languedoc appeared in London. By the summer of 1708, the prophets had attracted two hundred followers, among whom were others who laid claim to prophecy and to the working of miracles. They called themselves children of God, but their opponents knew them collectively as the French Prophets. This is a study of the nature of the opposition to the French Prophets.

Critics addressed themselves to two central questions: is ostensibly religious behavior explicable in the same way as all other human behavior? how can we explain the social appeal and resilience of extravagant behavior prompted by and grounded upon inspirations we know to be false? Answers to these questions were couched as often in medical as in theological terms. Science in the early seventeenth century had not customarily been called upon to supply paradigms for understanding religious behavior.[1] The physicalist models adopted by many critics of the French Prophets were basic to the revised boundaries of acceptable religious expression in early eighteenth-century England. While refuting the claims of the French Prophets to true prophecy and miracle, critics chose arguments that reveal the extent to which legitimate avenues of religious expression were being narrowed. When they came to define spiritual excitement as a function of internal fluid mechanics, when they

1. But see, for example, the use to which Hobbes put Galilean science in his explanation of human political behavior: Thomas A. Spragens, Jr., *The Politics of Motion: The World of Thomas Hobbes* (Lexington, Ky., 1973).

1

came to expect a reasonable continuity of style from the forms of daily intercourse to the forms of worship, critics undercut the value of religious ritual. As they denied the probability of new inspiration and new miracle, critics carried forward that restriction of publicly expressive piety against which the Wesleys would soon react.

A century of political crisis and wide-ranging Christian controversy yielded compelling reasons for England's most literate citizens to be concerned with the regimen of religious behavior. By the 1620s, Puritans and High Churchmen had recognized the implications of their theologies for political ideology, of their forms of worship for forms of government, of their standards of devotional expression for the civil laws which protect and incidentally define the individual. The Civil War between 1640 and 1648 was fought in part upon the strength of Christian millenarian visions. The disparate and contentious groups that arose then and shortly after as advocates of extensive sovereignty for prophecy, inspiration, and mystical insight were later regarded as evidence of political and social incoherence. Once Charles II had been restored and the Anglican Church Settlement reached (1660–62), men and women of settled convictions had to account for the breach between religious and social codes so manifest in the recent antinomianism of the Diggers, Ranters, early Quakers, Baptists, and Muggletonians.[2]

Political, social, and scientific suspicions of the disorderly and unpredictable lay just behind contemporary explanations for and arguments against erratic religious behavior. The English medical world struggled to account for physical symptoms supposedly motivated by strong Christian belief but so immediately disruptive and potentially subversive that no Christian state could comfortably ignore them. From the distress of the religious conflicts before the Restoration and from the stress of the political dissatisfactions that lingered on until the succession of the Hanoverian kings was finally secured, there developed a medical literature, partly philosophical,

2. On millenarianism before 1660, see John F. Wilson, *Pulpit in Parliament: Puritanism during the English Civil Wars, 1640–1648* (Princeton, 1969); William L. Lamont, *Godly Rule: Politics and Religion, 1603–60* (London, 1969); Peter Toon, ed., *Puritans the Millennium and the Future of Israel: Puritan Eschatology 1600 to 1660* (London, 1970); Christopher Hill, *Antichrist in Seventeenth Century England* (London, 1971); Charles Webster, *The Great Instauration: Science, Medicine and Reform 1626–1660* (New York, 1976); Bernard S. Capp, *The Fifth Monarchy Men: A Study in Seventeenth-Century Millenarianism* (London, 1972); Arthur L. Morton, *The World of the Ranters* (London, 1970); Melvin B. Endy, Jr., *William Penn and Early Quakerism* (Princeton, 1973).

devoted to an analysis of the diseases of intense religion. How could men and women accept prophecies and lead lives so far from normal that most social values were distorted, or believe themselves to be inspired and welcome physical convulsions? Physicians and philosophers reasoned from the processes of the physical body to the body politic; although the analogy was not new, seventeenth-century concepts of physical forces gave it a new significance.

England after the Restoration hosted a scientific circle as sensitive to its status in the European intellectual world as literate political English society was to its redemptive role among the European nations. Advances in the chemical and physical sciences and mathematics did not shutter off the millenarian perspectives of the previous era, but just as the natural philosophers such as Boyle, Hooke, and Newton sought the physical laws of universal stability, so they preferred an individual religious behavior as socially acceptable and balanced as the physical universe demanded of particulate matter. The analogy between religious action and physical law was tacit, but the application of the pattern of physical laws to problems of providence and teleology was made openly. Those among the clergy who accepted the Newtonian view of nature integrated Newtonian assumptions about society with a Low-Church (Latitudinarian) position, postulating a stabilizing role for the Church in the forwarding of Christian revelation and redemption. Prophecy was to be an ordered and ecclesiastical act of scriptural interpretation; there was no ecstasy.[3]

Prophecy was of special concern, for the instances of prophecy did not disappear with Oliver Cromwell's Commonwealth. For decades after the final efforts of the Fifth Monarchists to institute a New Jerusalem in London in 1661, the voices of other prophets were abroad in the land. As Independents, Quakers, Baptists, or followers

3. Margaret C. Jacob, *The Newtonians and the English Revolution, 1689–1720* (Ithaca, 1976), and "The Church and the Formulation of the Newtonian World-View," *Journal of European Studies* 1 (1971):128–48; David C. Kubrin, "Providence and the Mechanical Philosophy: the Creation and Dissolution of the World in Newtonian Thought. A Study of the Relations of Science and Religion in Seventeenth Century England" (Ph.D. diss., Cornell University, 1968); Richard S. Westfall, *Science and Religion in 17th Century England* (New Haven, 1958); Barbara J. Shapiro, "Latitudinarianism and Science," *Past and Present* 40 (1968):16–41, and "Science, Politics and Religion," *Past and Present* 66 (1975):133–38, with rejoinder by Lotte Mulligan, for whose articles see "Civil War Politics, Religion and the Royal Society," *Past and Present* 59 (1973):92–116, and "Anglicanism, Latitudinarianism, and Science in Seventeenth Century England," *Annals of Science* 30 (1973):213–19.

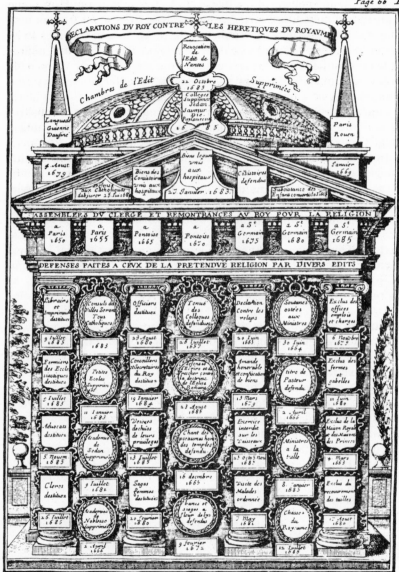

"Declarations du Roy contre les Heretiques du Royaume." Page from unidentified book, Musée du Désert.

of John Mason in 1694, they took up a less political but all the same fervid preaching of apocalyptic tidings.[4] If prophets were to come to England who not only knew the millenarian slogans but also had all the extravagant physical signs of inspiration, who deserved respect as leaders of a faithful Protestant remnant against the tyranny of the Pope and the French king, and who claimed to have the miraculous powers of true prophets, would not English society be most alert? Would not an especial effort be made to assess the new prophets? Would they not seem particularly threatening to a society which had, it was warmly hoped, found its balance?

In this monograph, I explore the English response to three such prophets. I will concentrate my discussion on the attempts of critics of all persuasions to explain the behavior and the rather wide appeal of these three religious figures and the group that grew around them. In the elaborate nature and large number of opposition writings, one can trace assumptions about religious behavior which are guides to early eighteenth-century beliefs about the nature of all human activity.

THE ORIGINS OF THE FRENCH PROPHETS

When the Huguenot Elie Marion left France in 1705, he carried with him a twenty-year tradition of miracle and prophecy. Ever since the Revocation of the Edict of Nantes in 1685, the French Protestants in southeastern France had heard angelic choirs in the sky, seen prophets weeping tears of blood, and witnessed their children predicting the fall of Babylon. In response to the mounting persecution after 1660, and, even more, to the expulsion of the Huguenot ministry at the Revocation, the faithful consoled themselves with the millenarian speculations of Pierre du Moulin, a pastor of the early part of the century, and, soon, his grandson, the pastor Pierre

4. See Christopher Hill,"John Mason and the End of the World," in his *Puritanism and Revolution* (London, 1969); Bernard Capp, "The Millennium and Eschatology in England," *Past and Present* 57 (1972):156–62; William L. Lamont, "Richard Baxter, The Apocalypse, and the Mad Major," *Past and Present* 55 (1972):68–90; Richard T. Vann, *The Social Development of English Quakerism 1655–1755* (Cambridge, Mass., 1969); Geoffrey T. Nuttall, "Overcoming the World: The Early Quaker Programme," in *Sanctity and Secularity: The Church and the World*, ed. Derek Baker (New York, 1973), p. 163; George H. Williamson, *Lodowick Muggleton* (London, 1919); Barry G. Reay, "The Muggletonians: A Study in Seventeenth-Century English Sectarianism," *Journal of Religious History* 9 (June 1976):32–49; P. G. Rogers, *The Fifth Monarchy Men* (London, 1966), pp. 110–33.

Jurieu, exiled in Rotterdam. Both men had calculated that the resurrection of the two witnesses of Revelation 11 would occur in 1689.[5] In illicit assemblies in Languedoc and Dauphiné, led by lay preachers (*prédicants*), many Huguenots persevered in their religious worship. Despite the threat of imprisonment or enslavement in galleys, they prayed together for an end to the persecution. But they also tended to view their prospective martyrdom as part of an accelerated millennial scheme. They heard sounds and voices in the winds of the mountainous Cévennes region: psalms, plaintive songs, tambourines beating as if soldiers marched to their rhythm.[6] The psalms seemed to serve a double purpose, as prelude to other promised rewards for the steadfast and as a goad to repentance for those who had wavered and possibly converted to Catholicism.

When the first prophets appeared among them in 1688, the Huguenots of this spiritual "Desert" (as they called it) exulted, for truly then, it seemed, were these the last days, and persecution could not last much longer. They prophesied while asleep. The physical act of prophecy was a metaphor: in the dead-but-not-dead state of the two witnesses of Revelation, in the full repose of the innocent, prophets were images of the True Church; as deliverance drew near, their bodies became agitated. The ecstasy of the first prophet, a sixteen-year-old shepherdess in Dauphiné, seemed at the beginning to be simply "a sort of Apoplexy, or Natural Lethargy, into which she fell without any appearance of a violent motion." Isabeau Vincent, baptized as a Catholic, had returned to the original Protestantism of her parents. On the night of February 3, 1688 (N.S.), asleep in the home of an uncle with whom she lived, she suddenly cried out and began to sing the Ten Commandments. Each night thereafter, when Huguenots sat in the room, she sang, preached, and prayed while asleep. Physicians examined her while she spoke; men sat by to copy down her words. Accounts of the prophet included detailed descriptions of the prophet's physical symptoms, for these were half the miracle and half the metaphor. Isabeau lay on her back and fell asleep swiftly. She sang the Ten

5. Pierre du Moulin, *Accomplissement des prophéties* (La Rochelle, 1612), pp. 239–41; [Pierre Jurieu], *Apologie pour l'accomplissement des prophéties* (Rotterdam, 1687), pp. 8–9; Charles Bost, *Les prédicants protestants des Cévennes et du Bas-Languedoc 1684–1700*, 2 vols. (Paris, 1912), 1:44, 49, 51, 178–80.

6. Pierre Jurieu, *Lettres pastorales addressées aux fidèles de France qui gémissent sous la captivité de Babylon* (Rotterdam, 1686); O. Douen, *Les premiers pasteurs du Désert (1685–1700)*, 2 vols. (Paris, 1879), 2:42.

Commandments in rhyme, then a psalm. After a pause, she preached fluently. Her gestures were as rapid as her speech, and sometimes that "Natural Lethargy" gave way to full bodily agitations. She woke in the morning refreshed and did not remember what had occurred during the night.[7] She became popular and widely known, and thus a distinct threat to the Catholic government. Imprisoned by royal officials in June 1688, the shepherdess soothed the distraught: others younger than she would appear as the Lord's prophets.

Within six months, younger and older prophets had indeed appeared in Dauphiné and Languedoc, fulfilling the words of Isabeau and of the prophecy of Joel repeated in Acts 2:17: "In the latter days your young people shall prophesy, and your old men shall dream dreams." The new prophets had physical symptoms which hinted at the emotional setting in which their visions flourished. Like Isabeau Vincent, they would be passive but agitated, asleep but awake, unconscious but perceptive, exhausted but refreshed. Their sermons and predictions betrayed a similar strain, a tension between mercy and judgment. When people gathered around them, they were equally impressed by the prophets' two-edged rhetoric and by their unusual physical state, evidence of the "hidden Manna" of the "Desert." The prophets were also a symbolic solution to the conflicting desires of the "Desert." Their existence was proof of religious continuity, yet they were surely heralds of spiritual transformation and a new era. Prophecy was consequently more than a substitute for professional preaching; it was a step forward and an implicit part of the millennial state.

After the bountiful harvest of 1688, throughout Dauphiné one might find young children prophesying. In the village near the home of Isabeau Vincent, more than sixty had received the Holy Spirit by the year's end. The sickness of one child was interpreted by his parents as the onset of the divine distemper of inspiration, where

7. Charles Bost, "Les 'Prophètes des Cévennes' au XVIIIe siècle," *Revue d'histoire et de philosophie religieuses* 5 (1925):403–4, 408–19; Justin Brun-Durand, "Vincent (Isabeau) dit la Bergère de Crest," *Dictionnaire biographique et biblio-iconographique de la Drôme*, 2 vols. (Grenoble, 1901), 2:403–4; Pierre Jurieu, *The Reflections of the Reverend and Learned Monsieur Jurieu, upon the Strange and Miraculous Exstasies of Isabel Vincent* (London, 1689); E. Arnaud, *Histoire des Protestants de Dauphiné aux XVIe, XVIIe et XVIIIe siècles*, 3 vols. (Paris, 1875–76), 3:71–74.

persons felt a drowsiness (*assoupissement*) and fell as if dead. Others followed comparable paths, fasting, not speaking for the three and one-half days mentioned in Revelation in regard to the two witnesses, or falling in a faint. By January 1689, as prophecy spread from Dauphiné into Languedoc, the *inspirés* became more public, more violent, and apparently more irresistible. With judgment looming in this apocalyptic year, the preliminary agitations of the inspired matched in violence the anticipated suffering of the wicked and the victory of the faithful. Enemies who perceived plots and artifices said that a glassmaker taught children to "beat their hands on their heads, to throw themselves down on the ground on their backs, to close their eyes, to puff up their stomachs and throats, to rest unresisting in this state for some moments, and then, waking with a start, to spout out anything that came to their mouths." The myth of the glassmaker, shaping children into prophets as one might blow glass, has been discredited, but this description of physical symptoms was generally accurate. Shaking, falling, choking, and convulsions would characterize future *inspirés* and also the prophets in London.[8]

As visions proliferated, as Judgment Day approached, the uninspired too fell to the ground in "Desert" congregations. This was a public act of repentance and a visible demonstration of faith. The prophets themselves—often awake and appearing in public— maintained an environment in which physical actions had spiritual values. Some Catholics claimed that the convulsions and fainting were symptomatic not of inspiration but of emotional contagion. The faithful did not shy from the metaphor of contagion but rather welcomed the divine epidemic. One sought the disease by fasting; one dared not risk the humiliation of immunity. The prophet Gabriel Astier had spread the disease by mouth, kissing children and giving them their new vocation. The faithful seemed to take literally the

8. *Copie d'une lettre de Genève touchant les enfans qui prophétisent en Dauphiné, en date du 25 décembre 1688* (The Hague, 1689); *A Relation of Several Hundreds of Children and Others that Prophesie and Preach in their Sleep* (London, 1689); *Histoire admirable de ce qui est arrivé dès le 12 novembre 1688 à Mornas en Dauphiné* (n.p., 1689); Bost, "Les 'Prophètes des Cévennes' au XVIIIe siècle," p. 405; David Augustin de Brueys, *Histoire du fanatisme de notre tems*, vol. 1 (1692), reprinted in *Archives curieuses de l'histoire de France*, ed. F. Danjou, 2d ser. (Paris, 1840), 11:347 (quote). The glassmaker myth is disproved in Cilette Blanc, "Genève et les origines du mouvement prophétique en Dauphiné et dans les Cévennes," *Revue d'histoire suisse* 23 (1942):234–49, but cf. Ronald Knox, *Enthusiasm* (Oxford, 1950), p. 358, for the metaphor.

breath of the mighty wind of Acts 2:2 which brought the Spirit on the day of Pentecost.[9]

"But their Apostate Brethren and those of the Communion of Rome not being able to hear that Voice which did Condemn them and which Called unto them, Repent, Repent, did stir up a Dreadful Persecution," wrote the French Prophets years later. In the winter and early spring of 1689, royal officials hunted down and imprisoned all prophets they could find, sent the young to convents or prison-hospitals, and condemned others to death. This too the prophets had foreseen, the short but cruel peak of persecution that would herald final deliverance. In April 1689, most prophets silent or secret, Judgment Day did not arrive as promised, but William and Mary were crowned joint Protestant sovereigns of England, just three and one-half years after the Revocation of the Edict of Nantes.[10]

Neither chiliasm nor prophecy disappeared from the "Desert" in the subsequent years. To the successes of William III of England and the Grand Alliance against France were attached dreams of the defeat of Catholic forces and the complete restoration of Huguenot freedoms. The few prophets who remained, hidden in the mountains of the Cévennes or in the Vivarais just to the north, preserved the rhetoric and hopes of the inspired of 1688. Late in 1700, a young man named Daniel Raoux discovered that God had "transfused into him" the spirit of the Old Testament prophet Daniel. Through Daniel and others in the Vivarais, the prophetic tradition was reasserted so widely and quickly that by the autumn of 1701 there were literally hundreds of prophets.[11]

9. For Catholics on contagion, see Valentin Esprit Fléchier, *Lettres choisies* (Paris, 1752), 1:357, and de Brueys, *Histoire du fanatisme*, p. 366. On contagion among the Huguenots, see Bost, "Les 'Prophètes des Cévennes' au XVIIIe siècle," pp. 417–18; *Histoire admirable*, p. 17; Bibl. Nîmes, MSS 186 (15), p. 400.

10. Stack MSS lj: Historical Relation, fol. 7; Pierre Jurieu, *Lettres pastorales* (Rotterdam, 1688/89), pp. 492–517.

11. Charles Bost, "Les 'prophètes' du Languedoc en 1701 et 1702," *Revue historique* 136 (1921):10–12; Bost, *Les prédicants*, 2:305. The first royal proclamation specifically against Languedoc *fanatiques* (*inspirés* and their followers) was printed on June 15, 1701 (N.S.), and began, "Le Roy ayant esté informé que depuis quelque temps il s'est trouvé dans le Diocèse d'Usez ou Lieux voisin, des gens qui affectent de paroistre Fanatiques dans le dessein de troubler le repos Public . . ." (Archives de l'Hérault [Montpellier], MSS C.180, fol. 325). David Flotard, in F.-Maximilien Misson's *Le théâtre sacré des Cévennes* (London, 1707), p. 62, claimed that the designation "fanatique" was arrived at by the medical faculty of the University of Montpellier after an examination of the *inspirés*. There is no evidence whatsoever to support this. The term "fanatique" had been current at least since 1650 as a general description of what the English were calling an "enthusiast." See Walther von

In addition to recurrent millennial themes announced more boldly than ever before, the "Desert" was now backdrop for miracles more dramatic than voices in the sky. Pierre Chantagrel walked barefoot but unharmed over burning coals; newborn infants spoke up to refuse Catholic baptism; Jeanne Bonnisolle promised that she would die and then rise an hour later. (She fainted but did not die.) In September 1701, Marie Boîteuse wept tears of blood. An *inspiré* standing by said that the blood was a demand for repentance and a sign that the world would soon come to an end.[12]

The inspired also became more aggressive. Isabeau Dauphinenche, terrifying the witnesses who testified against her as a *fanatique*, prayed in court for the conversion of her judges. Women and children of Valérargues rescued a captured *inspiré* from three priests. Led by him to the village church, they destroyed the altar and smashed the crucifix.[13]

By November 1701, as more prophets arose in the plains of Bas-Languedoc and in the Cévennes, over three hundred and fifty *fanatiques* were in prison, and the Intendant Bâville had condemned some forty prophets to slavery in the galleys. Even so, a royal officer that month could come across the inhabitants of Ayguesvives dressed as if for a holiday on a normal workday, standing in the road listening to a fourteen-year-old boy sing psalms and preach.[14]

Early in 1702, an itinerant troop of *inspirés* and friends had gathered in the mountains of the Cévennes, fugitives from the severe justice of priests and soldiers. They brought the breath of the divine spirit with them as they toured the countryside, and they prophesied violently against their enemies. Among them was Abraham Mazel, aged twenty-four, who on July 22, 1702 (N.S.), under frantic agitations, pronounced the divine order to take up arms without delay

Wartburg, "Fanatisme" and "Fanatique," in *Französisches Etymologisches Wörterbuch* (Berlin, 1934), 3:409; Paul Robert, "Fanatique," in *Dictionnaire alphabétique et analogique de la langue française* (Paris, 1955), 2:1909.

12. Archives de l'Hérault (Montpellier), MSS C.180, fols. 321v., 328v.–329, MSS C.181, fols. 28v.–30, 116, 125v., 128, 168; Bost, "Les 'prophètes' du Languedoc en 1701 et 1702," 136:8, 31, and 137 (1921):2.

13. Archives de l'Hérault (Montpellier), MSS C.180, fol. 415, MSS C.181, fols. 505, 520; Bost, "Les 'prophètes' du Languedoc en 1701 et 1702," 136:17, 20, 26; Ernest Roschach, ed., *Histoire générale de Languedoc*, 16 vols. (Toulouse, 1872–1915), vol. 14, "pièces justificatives," no. 569, cols. 1537–41.

14. Bost, "Les 'prophètes' du Languedoc en 1701 et 1702," 136:19–21; Roschach, *Histoire générale de Languedoc*, vol. 14, no. 580, cols. 1555–56, no. 613, col. 1608; Archives Nationales (Paris), AN 154 Ap II 120, Fonds Lamoignon de Basville, pièce 37, letter of Nov. 4, 1701 (N.S.).

and rescue Huguenots imprisoned at Pont-de-Montvert. Other *inspirés* confirmed the order. On July 24, twelve days after France had entered the War of the Spanish Succession against England and her Protestant allies, some forty to sixty Huguenots, carrying an assortment of guns and makeshift weapons, began their guerilla war against the military and clerical authorities of Languedoc and Dauphiné. So began the revolt of the Camisards.[15]

Their numbers increased to five hundred by September, with eighty under the leadership of the famous twenty-year-old prophet "Colonel" Jean Cavalier. Among the thousand or more men and women who entered the guerilla bands in 1703 were three whose names will figure prominently among the French Prophets in London: Durand Fage, Elie Marion, and Jean Cavalier of Sauve (not to be confused with the "Colonel"). By 1704, the Camisards had a force of perhaps two thousand men and women.[16]

The war proper lasted more than two years, from 1702 through much of 1704. Twenty thousand royal troops did not have immediate success against these bands of Huguenots who knew the mountains, caves, and footpaths of the Cévennes as they knew their psalms. Moreover, the soldiers were battling men and women who were divinely warned of traitors, guided to their camps at night by celestial lights, and protected from ambush by guardian angels.[17] Many of the Camisard leaders were themselves prophets; uninspired commanders relied upon prophets among their troops.

Fearing the consequences of this prolonged revolt, especially since nearby Savoy had in October 1703 allied itself with the English and Dutch who had been making efforts to provide the Camisards with supplies, Louis XIV sent the distinguished Claude Louis Hector, duc de Villars, Maréchal de France, to direct the royal troops in Languedoc. Villars arrived in April 1704, several days after "Colonel" Cavalier's forces had sustained a severe defeat including loss of stores and ammunition. Villars promptly offered a general

15. The term "Camisard" is derived either from the word for "night attack" (obs. Fr. *camisade*) or from the patois for a white shirt (*camisole*). See Charles Bost, ed., "Mémoires inédits d'Abraham Mazel et d'Elie Marion sur la guerre des Cévennes, 1701–1708," vol. 34 of *Publications de la Société Huguenote de Londres* (1931), p. 30. Cf. Frank Puaux, "Origines, causes, et conséquences de la guerre des Camisards," *Revue historique* 129 (1918):212, 235.

16. Bost, "Mémoires inédits," pp. 21–24; Misson, *Théâtre sacré*, p. 87; Marcel Pin, *Jean Cavalier* (Nîmes, 1936), pp. 6–8.

17. Bost, "Mémoires inédits," pp. 18, 20, 30; Misson, *Théâtre sacré*, pp. 28, 34, 38, 107.

amnesty to all rebels who would surrender, then combined diplomacy with wholesale imprisonment of the parents and relatives of the remaining Camisards, a strategy which proved effective. Finding the Cévennes ravaged, their families jailed, their supplies exhausted, their friends and prophets executed, and fresh royal troops always at their heels, band after band of Camisards surrendered between May and November 1704. Elie Marion and fellow prophets sought the advice of the Spirit, for they could not abandon a divinely inspired war without a specific divine command. At length he and his companions understood the silence of the Spirit as itself a command to surrender, and most of them, like so many others, took advantage of the general treaty conditions to make their way to Geneva.[18]

Unlike most, however, Elie Marion returned in 1705 to fight once more, spurred on by English agents in Switzerland. Supplied feebly by England and the United Provinces, the Camisards who continued the battle achieved little. The duc de Berwick, successor to Villars, caught many of the remaining prophets and rounded up a large circle of supporters in Nîmes. Marion capitulated a second time and returned to Switzerland in August 1705 with Durand Fage and Abraham Mazel. Stray bands of rebels and *inspirés* still hid in the Cévennes "as a leaven," and Mazel himself would engage in sporadic guerilla actions until his death in 1710, but the harsh war was over.[19]

The mimetic violence and peace of the act of prophecy had been since 1688 a figure for the spiritual agitations of individual Huguenots, for the ambivalence of Calvinist mercy and judgment, for the social predicament of the "Desert." With the outbreak of the rebellion, the physical motions of the prophets served as a prototype

18. Charles Alméras, *La révolte des Camisards* (Paris, 1960), pp. 175–77, 182–86; Mme. de Merez, in *Mémoire*, ed. E. Marie, comte de Barthélemy (n.p., 1874), "Résumé des événements survenus dans les Cévennes et le Diocèse de Nîmes de 1688 à 1704," pp. 134–43; Philippe de Courcillon, marquis de Dangeau, *Journal*, ed. Soulié et al., 19 vols. (Paris, 1854–60), 9:492–93; Claude Louis Hector, duc de Villars, *Vie . . . écrite par lui-même*, ed. M. Anquetil, 4 vols. (Paris, 1785), 1:299–300; idem., *Mémoires*, ed. le marquis de Vogüé, 6 vols. (Paris, 1884–1904), vol. 2, Appendix, p. 319; Bost, "Mémoires inédits," pp. 61–88.
19. Bost, "Mémoires inédits," pp. 89–142, 196–200, 206–14; Antoine Court, *Histoires des troubles des Cévennes*, 3 vols. (Villefranche, 1760), 3:123–29; Dangeau, *Journal*, 10:135, 210; Alméras, *La révolte des Camisards*, pp. 223–25; Stack MSS lj; Historical Relation, fol. 21. Cf. C. G. Sturgill, *Marshall Villars and the War of the Spanish Succession* (Lexington, Ky., 1965).

for social violence: just as heavy breathing, gasping and choking,
flailing of limbs, convulsions, and falling as if dead were pre-
monitory signs of true inspiration, so the grim battles of the
Camisards were a necessary preliminary to the restoration of the
True Church. The prophets reversed the direction of prophetic ritual
from its inward reflection of the body politic through the medium of
the physical body to direct action upon the body politic through the
power of *inspirés*. The prophets thus had the momentum to break
the taboo against generalized violence which in the forms of
royalism and pacifism had prevailed among the Huguenots of
Languedoc since 1630.[20]

However much English society might admire stubborn Protestant
guerillas, however much it might be willing to accept the possibility
of miracle and inspiration for the persecuted martyrs in desperate
need of divine aid, religious behavior which drew its validity from a
setting of war and despair would seem inappropriate in London, in
the sitting rooms to which came Durand Fage, Jean Cavalier of
Sauve, and Elie Marion. Yet some in England in 1706 could find new
meaning in that behavior, new hope in the scarred language of
Cévenol prophecy.

THE FRENCH PROPHETS IN ENGLAND

At the center of an increasingly stable and powerful financial world,
at the heart of an increasingly urban economy, with a population of
about half a million, London in its wealth, size, and diversity presented the Camisard *inspirés* with a milieu far different from that to
which they were accustomed. England's lesser gentry were becom-
ing city folk and mingled, if only occasionally, with both the
merchant oligarchy of London and the less secure, more crowded
artisans and laborers. Virtuosi and penmen met at coffeehouses to
read foreign and domestic newspapers, to debate the virtues and
dangers of religious nonconformity, the conduct of the continental

20. Cf. Mary Douglas, *Purity and Danger* (London, 1966), pp. 128 ff.; Kenelm
Burridge, *New Heaven, New Earth: A Study of Millenarian Activities* (Oxford, 1969),
p. 61; Peter L. Berger, *The Sacred Canopy* (New York, 1967), pp. 38–40. On the
royalism of the Huguenots, see especially Guy H. Dodge, *The Political Theory of the
Huguenots of the Dispersion, with Special Reference to the Thought and Influence of
Pierre Jurieu* (New York, 1947); Philippe Joutard, "Les Camisards: 'Prophètes de la
Grande Révolution' ou derniers combattants des guerres de religion?" in *L'esprit
républicain, Colloque d'Orléans 4-5 Septembre 1970*, présentée par J. Viard (Paris, 1972),
pp. 113–16.

war against France, or the role of miracle in the natural universe. The coffeehouses were a by-product of English commercial and colonial expansion through control of the seas, the newspapers a sign of the rather widespread literacy in London, and the debates characteristic of a literate, prosperous society given to controversy. Whigs still feared that their "Glorious" Revolution of 1688, which replaced the Catholic James II with the Protestants William and Mary, would be overturned by Jacobites upon the death of Queen Anne, but in 1706 it was more the fear of popery than the fear of political insurrection that informed the passions of the London citizen.[21]

The differences between London and the Cévennes were not necessarily handicaps to the diffusion of prophecy or to the growth of a religious group focused on three refugee prophets. One could move relatively freely through the city. One could make contact with an enormously diverse collection of Christian cohorts. One could print inspirations with more facility than in France, and with some assurance that one's audience could read. Above all, and most important at the very beginning, as a Huguenot one could locate oneself in an often familiar society of forty or fifty thousand other refugees clustered in the capital.[22]

The *inspirés* found their first receptive audience among refugees from Languedoc and also in the persons of the marquis de Miremont and his secretary, Charles Portales, who had been involved in

21. For this general background, see P. G. M. Dickson, *The Financial Revolution in England* (London and New York, 1967); Alan Everitt, *Change in the Provinces: the Seventeenth Century* [Dept. of English Local History, Leicester University. Occasional Papers, 2d ser., no. 1] (Leicester, 1969); idem, "Social Mobility in Early Modern England," *Past and Present* 33 (1966:56–73; Christopher Clay, "The Price of Freehold Land in the Later Seventeenth and Eighteenth Century," *Economic History Review*, 2d ser. 27 (1974):173–89; J. H. Plumb, *The Growth of Political Stability in England 1675–1725* (London, 1967); F. M. L. Thompson, "The Social Distribution of Landed Property in England since the Sixteenth Century," *Economic History Review*, 2d ser. 19 (1966):505–17; Lawrence Stone, "Literacy and Education in England 1640–1900," *Past and Present* 42 (1969):69–139; David Cressy, "Literacy in Pre-industrial England," *Societas* 4 (1974):229–40; Richard T. Vann, "Literacy in Seventeenth-Century England: Some Hearth-Tax Evidence," *Journal of Interdisciplinary History* 5 (1974):287–93; D. W. Jones, "London Merchants and the Crisis of the 1690s," in *Crisis and Order in English Towns 1500–1700. Essays in Urban History*, ed. Peter Clark and Paul Slack (Toronto, 1972), pp. 311–55; Arthur J. Weitzman, "Eighteenth-Century London: Urban Paradise or Fallen City," *Journal of the History of Ideas* 36 (1975):469–80.
22. Robin D. Gwynn, "The Distribution of Huguenot Refugees in England," *Proceedings of the Huguenot Society of London* 21 (1969):435.

English efforts to support and supply the Camisards.[23] Directed by
the Spirit to leave their occupations in Switzerland and go to
London, the three prophets were at first concerned primarily to
predict the defeat of the French and the ultimate victory of those
faithful who remained in Languedoc. To these predictions they
added the Spirit's assurance that soon they would set forth on
missions back to France. However, as new listeners appeared who
had less sympathy with the plight of the Camisards than they did
with the miracles and inspirations in the Cévennes as signs of an
approaching millennium, the prophets' stance shifted from that of
recruiters to that of heralds of apocalypse and preachers of
repentance.[24]

Of the new followers active by the spring of 1707, four deserve
individual mention, for their names will recur. Nicolas Fatio de
Duillier, born in 1664 to a bourgeois Huguenot family of Geneva,
had early established an international reputation as a mathematician
and as a disciple of Sir Isaac Newton. Along with the lawyer Jean
Daudé, Fatio took upon himself the task of transcribing the
prophecies of the inspired.[25] François-Maximilien Misson, in his late
forties, was a Huguenot gentleman, son of a refugee minister, and
author of the popular A New Voyage to Italy; he took as his task a
compilation of accounts of émigrés who had witnessed prophecy
and miracle in the Cévennes.[26] John Lacy, a well-to-do English
Presbyterian, aged forty-two, completed the English translation of
Misson's collected testimonies and would himself soon become

23. On de Miremont and Portales, see Calendar of State Papers Domestic,
1703–1704, pp. 126–29; Abel Boyer, The History of the Reign of Queen Anne,
Digested into Annals. Year the Second (London, 1704), pp. 101–5; P. J. Shears,
"Armand de Bourbon, Marquis de Miremont," Proceedings of the Huguenot Society
of London 20 (1963):405–18; Bost, "Mémoires inédits," prefatory note by Major
Francis M. E. Kennedy, and p. 159n.

24. The most readily available account of this is in Bost, "Mémoires inédits." Cf.
Georges Ascoli, "L'affaire des prophètes français à Londres," Revue du XVIIIe
siècle 3 (1916):8–28, 85–109.

25. On Fatio, see Frank E. Manuel, A Portrait of Isaac Newton (Cambridge,
Mass., 1968), chap. 9; Charles A. Domson, "Nicolas Fatio de Duillier and the
Prophets of London: An Essay in the Historical Interaction of Natural Philosophy
and Millennial Belief in the Age of Newton" (Ph.D. diss., Yale University, 1972).

26. On Misson, see Public Record Office (London), MSS PROB. 11/584, no. 78,
Will of Maximilien Misson, Jan. 3, 1721; F.-Maximilien Misson, A New Voyage to
Italy, 2 vols. (London, 1695 [original French edition, The Hague, 1691]); Marc-
Auguste Borgeaud, "Maximilien Misson et les trophées de l'Escalade," Geneva, n.s.
1 (1953):133–35; J.-M. Quérard, Les supercheries littéraires dévoilées, 2d ed., 3 vols.
(Paris, 1869–70), 3:980e, as well as standard French biographical dictionaries.

inspired, later to assume practical leadership of the group.[27] Lacy's longtime friend, Sir Richard Bulkeley, second baronet, born in 1660, holder of a large estate in Ireland and a country house in Surrey, virtuoso and member of the Royal Society of Ireland, supported the publications of the group and contributed (with Misson) a substantial number of controversial writings in favor of the prophets.[28] The stature of these men and the public knowledge of their relationships with the *inspirés* gave prominence to the activities of the group. The transcriptions of Elie Marion's *Avertissemens* and Misson's *Théâtre sacré des Cévennes* were published in April 1707. In May, the English translations (*Prophetical Warnings* and *A Cry from the Desart*) appeared. By this time, the assorted French and English prophets and believers had become known collectively as the French Prophets.[29]

Despite expectations of enthusiastic reception from London Huguenots, the French Prophets had only twenty-four men and women in their orbit at the end of March 1707, after ten months of prophecy and informal advertisement. What had happened was that the Huguenot community, swayed by the consistories of the most powerful French Protestant churches, had been turned against Fage, Cavalier, and Marion. After a series of interviews and some exposure to the prophets in the act of prophecy, most of the leading Huguenot pastors had become actively hostile to the *inspirés*. The

27. For biographical material on Lacy, see Edmund Calamy, *An Historical Account of My Own Life*, ed. John T. Rutt, 2 vols. (London, 1829), 2:76–78, 94–99, 113–14; Walter Courtenay Pepys, comp., *Genealogy of the Pepys Family 1273–1887* (London, 1887), genealogical chart (John Lacy being the son of Jerome Lacy and Elizabeth Pepys); House of Lords Record Office, MSS 2519, Lacy's Estate Act, fols. 51–74, and Committee Book, Minutes 24 October 1704–5 April 1710, fols. 337–38. There is no satisfactory printed account of Lacy's life; the article in the *Dictionary of National Biography* (11:382–83) is taken from Calamy and Lacy's *Warnings* (1707).
28. On Bulkeley, see G. E. Cokayne, ed., *Complete Baronetage*, 4:207; K. Theodore Hoppen, *The Common Scientist in the Seventeenth Century* (London, 1970), passim; Dudley W. R. Bahlmann, *The Moral Revolution of 1688* (Hamden, Conn., 1968), pp. 19–21; *Dictionary of National Biography*, 3:233 (which gives the wrong birthdate). Many letters from Bulkeley to his physician Dr. Lister are at the Bodleian Library (Oxford); estate documents are at Bourne Hall, Ewell, Surrey, and at the Public Record Office, Dublin.
29. Elie Marion, *Avertissemens prophetiques* (London, 1707), was translated as Elias Marion, *Prophetical Warnings of Elias Marion* (London, 1707); Misson's *Théâtre sacré* was translated as *A Cry from the Desart: or, Testimonials of the miraculous Things lately come to pass in the Cévennes* (London, 1707). Exact dates of publication for these and all other works by the French Prophets and their opponents have been gleaned from announcements in newspapers.

hostility was due in part to the psychologically upsetting situation of refugee ministers whose guilt for having left their flocks in France made itself manifest on occasion in serious considerations of covert missions to the faithful. This guilt was exacerbated by the very presence of prophets who had substituted for the absent ministers and actually baptized infants and performed marriage ceremonies without ordination or recognized rank in the assembly of elders of official churches.[30] The hostility was due also to the precarious position of the Huguenots in the political environment of late Stuart England. Dependent upon the Whigs for toleration and financial support (relief monies for the poorer refugees), the Huguenot clergy could not risk tolerating prophets liable to predict, mime, or spark violence. Already disliked by London laborers who accused the Huguenot weavers in particular of stealing their livelihoods, soon to be accused of mismanaging refugee relief monies, Huguenot leaders were zealous to prevent incidents that would reflect poorly on their community.[31] On January 5, 1706/7, the Savoy consistory, followed by other consistories, published a condemnation of the three prophets. Ministers announced from their pulpits that "the Agitations of these pretended Prophets are only the Effect of a voluntary Habit, of which they are entirely Masters, though in their Fits they seem to be agitated by a Superior Cause. . . . But the Way in which they make the Spirit speak, is still more unworthy of him, which is by perpetual Hesitations, Childish Repetitions, unintelligible Stuff, gross Contradictions, manifest Lies, Conjectures turned into Predictions, already convicted of Falsehood by the Event; or some moral Precepts, which may be heard every day much better expressed, and have nothing new but the Grimaces, with which they are accompanied."[32]

30. Douen, *Les premiers pasteurs du Désert*, 1:134, 160–61; Archives of the Library of the French Protestant Church, Soho Square (London), MS 8, Threadneedle Street Church, "Livre des actes de 1692/3 à 1708," pp. 499–501; Fatio Calendar, Sept.–Oct. 1707; Marion, *Prophetical Warnings*, pp. 3–7; Misson, *Théâtre sacré*, pp. 143–46.

31. Roy A. Sundstrom, "Aid and Assimilation: A Study of the Economic Support Given French Protestants in England, 1688–1727" (Ph.D. diss., Kent State University, 1972), pp. 132–65, 185–88, 204–5, substantially summarized in his article, "French Huguenots and the Civil List, 1696–1727: A Study of Alien Assimilation in England," *Albion* 8 (1976):219–35; William A. Shaw, "The English Government and the Relief of Protestant Refugees," *English Historical Review* 9 (1894):346–51; P. Thornton and N. Rothstein, "The Importance of the Huguenots in the London Silk Industry," *Proceedings of the Huguenot Society of London* 20 (1964):87.

32. The original announcement, in French, is reprinted in full in Bost, "Mémoires

Unfortunately, this "Acte Noir," as the French Prophets termed it, inflamed the Huguenot populace, who now insulted the *inspirés* in public, spattered them with mud and filth, and assaulted them on their doorsteps.[33] The new persecution allowed the French Prophets to establish a tradition similar to yet independent of the Camisard experience, and the subsequent excommunication of the prophets by the consistories between March 30 and April 19 furthered the group's definition of its own boundaries. Two riots followed, as men and women chased the prophets and their followers from house to house. To avoid repetition of such events, the consistories encouraged legal action against Fatio, Daudé, and Elie Marion for publishing blasphemous and seditious prophecies in Marion's *Avertissemens*. In the warrant, Marion was described as a "pseudo-prophet, an abominable, detestable and diabolic blasphemer, a disturber of the peace, heretic and impostor, publisher of false, scandalous and seditious libels." The trial of the three men dragged on from May to November, but eventually the three were found guilty and sentenced to stand on a scaffold in Charing Cross and at the Royal Exchange. They had been unable to convince the jury that Marion's prophecies of destruction were spiritual metaphors, or that his inspirations were not the pride of a warrior.[34]

The Huguenot response to and eventual indictment of the *inspirés* hinted at most of the assessments of the prophets and their followers

---

inédits," p. 160. This translation is from N. N., *An Account of the Lives and Behaviour of the Three French Prophets* (London, 1708), pp. 9–10.

33. F.-Maximilien Misson, *Plainte et censure des calomnieuses accusations publiées par le Sieur Claude Groteste de la Motte* (London, 1708), p. 52.

34. On the original legal action against the three French Prophets, see Bost, "Mémoires inédits," pp. 158–65; Misson, *Théâtre sacré*, pp. vii, 146; Fatio Calendar, April 1–May 5, 1707; *Account of the Apprehending and Taking Six French Prophets* [broadside] (London, 1707); "Relation historique de ce qui s'est passé à Londres au sujet des Prophètes Camisards," *Nouvelles de la république des lettres* (February 1708), pp. 132–33; Richard Kingston, *Enthusiastick Impostors No Divinely Inspired Prophets*, 2 parts (London, 1707, 1709), 2:219–20; Stack MSS lj: Historical Relation, fol. 29. Ascoli, "L'affaire des prophètes français à Londres," p. 85, cites the warrant, which I have not located. I have translated the warrant's description of Marion from Ascoli's French. The warrant was based on the statute of Elizabeth I.15, "An act against fond and fantastical prophesies." On the final trial, sentence, and punishment, see especially Fatio Calendar, November–December 1707; Stack MSS lg: Récit abrégé, pp. 47–48, 62, and Stack MSS lj: Historical Relation, fol. 32; *English Post*, no. 1119, December 1–3, 1707; *Post-Boy*, no. 1957, November 29–December 2, 1707; B.P.U.G., MSS fr. 602, fols. 115–115v.; Narcissus Luttrell, *A Brief Historical Relation of State Affairs from September 1678 to April 1714*, 6 vols. (Oxford, 1857), 6:239–40.

that would appear in the English controversial literature. But events were to come, associated much more with the English among the French Prophets, which would figure prominently in opposition tracts. Before I can move on to the central concerns of this study, I must outline those events and paint in some of the background.

The French Prophets in London did not simply bring the issue of inspiration immediately and physically to the attention of the English. In the summer of 1707, they also brought before the public the knotty problem of miracles. Undaunted by daily persecution and legal prosecution, growing in numbers, they seemed also to be growing in the gifts of the Lord. Again, they would develop and foster a religious tradition parallel to but independent of the Cévennes.

The spring and summer of 1707 were filled with reports of the severe English defeat at Almanza in Spain and the possibility of another war in the Baltic that might disrupt English naval supplies. Parliament had passed the bill for the Union of Scotland and England, which came into effect on May 1. Despite general economic prosperity, there was a mild financial panic and a sharp increase in the number of bankruptcies.[35] Political uneasiness with the conduct of the war against France was mounting, and in a moment with unforeseen consequences for court and country, Sarah Churchill, wife of the duke of Marlborough, introduced Abigail Hill (Mrs. Masham) to Queen Anne. Within two years Anne would give major support to the Tory cause, and the Whigs—upon whose good will the Huguenot community relied—would find themselves considerably weakened. In this atmosphere of political maneuvering and economic anxiety, John Lacy, inspired, began to speak in tongues.

The tongue was Latin, and not all were convinced that this proved the divine source of Lacy's prophetic calling. For this was the issue: how could one recognize a true prophet (whose doctrine was consistent with Scripture but not at all new) except by the signs of his/her mission? Admitting theological flexibility and the fact that they did not come to preach a new set of beliefs, the French Prophets were constrained by both Camisard antecedent and Christian logic to welcome miracles that should be evidence for true inspiration. Significantly, the miracles the French Prophets did

35. T. S. Ashton, *Economic Fluctuations in England 1700–1800* (Oxford, 1959), p. 116.

begin to claim were not broadly social and public but private, personal, and explicitly physical. The exorbitant agitations of the inspired were confirmed by miracles of the mouth and body, so that later critics could with facility apply medical analogies to both inspiration and miracle. Sir Richard Bulkeley, the day after Lacy first spoke in Latin, immediately prepared for opposition to the essential privacy of the miracle: "If Mr. Lacy had spoken any *modern* Language, Men would then have objected, that he had learned it perhaps by Travel, or by Converse with those of that Language; and now that he has spoken in a Language which no Country speaks, it will be objected, that the Spirit of Wisdom would not be the Author of a *Miracle* to no Purpose, to make a Man speak a Language that none other speak, or may be converted in. Thus do Men fight against even all the sensible Demonstrations of the Goodness of God to them."[36] This was on July 3. At the end of July, Lacy, "under ecstasy," glided ten feet across the floor of the room in which he prophesied. The same day, the English prophet Betty Gray, a young woman of sixteen, predicted that Lacy would receive the gift of healing. In August, according to believers, Lacy did indeed cure Betty Gray of a temporary blindness.[37]

Possible opposition to the terms and definitions of these miracles was supplemented at the same time by the increased opportunity for criticism of false prophecy and improper behavior. Lacy had prophesied that the guns of the Tower of London would roar by mid-August, but they were silent. Lacy and Gray had been involved in agitated warnings dealing with the whore of Babylon (whose defeat was performed in mime) and the morning star (whose brightness was embraced by Lacy). The false prophecy and the dramatic representations became notorious, and sexual innuendos against the prophets appeared in enemy tracts.[38]

During this period, however, the prophets' new powers and promises had attracted a wider following whose very presence

36. Kingston, *Enthusiastick Impostors*, 2:75; compare the reactions of several ministers to their meeting with the French Prophets on July 2 (1:61): "Mr. Y[at]es had not altered his Mind, upon the uttering of Latin. Mr. K[eit]h had more to say to lessen the Credit of the supposed *Inspirations* being from the Spirit of God. Mr. W[oodcoc]k also was scandalized at Mr. Lacy's *Whistling* when under his *Ecstatic* Motions."
37. Fatio Calendar, July 30, 1707; Lacy, *Warnings*, 1:100, 2:21–22, 26–27, 39–40, 55, 64–66.
38. Lacy, *Warnings*, 2:7–8, 171–72, 178, 3:6–7; Kingston, *Enthusiastick Impostors*, 1:65–66.

seemed to give the group the confidence to gloss over false inspiration. Among the new followers were fifteen or twenty English Philadelphians, men and women influenced by the mystical principles of Jakob Boehme as interpreted by Jane Lead (d. 1704) and by Richard Roach, an Anglican clergyman interested in alchemy and spiritual transformation. Theirs had been an inward search for revelation and the true peace of Philadelphia, but they rather quickly identified the Camisard prophets and their English heirs as another valid Christian dispensation leading to the millennial state.[39] Gradually their quietist inclinations and forms would make themselves felt among the French Prophets, and their role helps account for the changes in the group in its final years. Of more direct concern to this study, their adherence was noted by opponents as typical of the motley collection of Baptists, Quakers, Presbyterians, Anglicans, and experienced seekers involved in a religious group whose criteria for membership were in fact unclear. Alarm at the wide appeal of the French Prophets stemmed as much from the ambiguous boundaries of the group (theological, social, economic) as from the particular actions and predictions of its inspired leaders.[40]

As the French Prophets spread, with "50 or 60 English in London" who had the preliminary signs of inspiration by November 1707, so the number of opposition tracts increased.[41] And there was

39. For background on the Philadelphians, see Serge Hutin, *Les disciples anglais de Jacob Boehme aux XVIIe et XVIIIe siècles* (Paris, 1960); Nils Thune, *The Behmenists and the Philadelphians* (Uppsala, 1948); D. P. Walker, *The Decline of Hell* (London, 1964); Richard Roach, *The Great Crisis* (London, 1725 [*sic* for 1727]). The relationship between the French Prophets and the Philadelphians is best traced in the Bodleian Library (Oxford), Rawlinson MSS D.1152–57, Diary of Richard Roach, and MSS D.832–33, Papers of Richard Roach, as well as MSS D.1318, fols. 52–68.

40. Cf. Kingston, *Enthusiastick Impostors*, 2:132–33: "The whole *Gang* of them, generally speaking, are composed of *Atheists, Papists, Quakers Anti-Scripturists, Socinians, Ranters, Muggletonians, and Debauchees*; for though other Sects and Factions have some *Terms* and *Qualifications* requisite to the Admission of Members into their Societies; these pretended Prophets have none at all, but Tag, Rag, Knave or Fool, Rich, or Poor, young Children, or superannuated Dotards, as soon as they come among them, are *blessed, admitted*, and immediately set up for Prophets; so that, instead of admiring (as some do) that there are so many of them, I wonder there are no more, since, like *Hell*, they refuse none." Actually, the majority of the English followers were probably Anglican, and I find no Muggletonians or Ranters in the group. "Atheists," "Anti-Scripturists," and "Debauchees" are general terms of reproach, but there is some evidence that Thomas Emes had once been a Socinian (denying the orthodox concept of the Trinity): Regents Park College (Oxford), Angus Library, Cripplegate [Baptist] Congregation Church Book 1699–1724, fol. 8 (September 1694).

41. By mid-November, more than twenty-five tracts, broadsides, and newspaper articles critical of the French Prophets had been published in London.

much to talk about, for on October 12, Lacy intimated that God's servants would raise the dead.[42] Before the date for the raising was set, Lacy had restored the vision of James Jackson, and Richard Roach had cured Betty Gray of a dumbness of voice. In December, three weeks after Fatio, Daudé, and Marion had suffered public humiliation on the scaffold, Dr. Thomas Emes, an English follower who had occasionally been inspired, died. During Emes's sickness, Lacy had prophesied, "If thou diest, I will raise thee; or if thou remainest, for some time, as thou art, I will restore thee." A week after Emes was buried in Bunhill Fields, the English prophet John Potter finally set the specific date for the resurrection: May 25, 1708.[43]

In anticipation of the conclusive miraculous proof of the truth of the French Prophets' dispensation, various inspired members and their scribes set off on missions to towns near London: Enfield, Colchester, and Ipswich.[44] These missions and the well-known prophecies about Dr. Emes contributed much to the public recognition of the English set of French Prophets. The English now had trouble with their own churches, as the Huguenots had had troubles with the consistories. Edmund Calamy preached against the French Prophets while John Lacy, staunch Presbyterian, sat listening in his pew.[45] Quakers of the Peel Meeting (London) dissociated them-

42. Lacy, *Warnings*, 3:169–70; *A Collection of Prophetical Warnings of the Eternal Spirit* (London, 1708), pp. 73, 78.

43. Bodleian Library (Oxford), Rawlinson MSS D.1152, fol. 92; John Lacy, *A Relation of the Dealings of God to his Unworthy Servant John Lacy, Since the Time of his Believing and Professing himself Inspired* (London, 1708), p. 24; Sir Richard Bulkeley, *An Answer to Several Treatises lately published on the Subject of the Prophets* (London, 1708), pp. 113–14; *Predictions concerning the Raising the Dead Body of Mr. Thomas Emes* (London, 1708), pp. 1, 2, 8; Fatio Calendar, December 25, 1707.

44. Fatio Calendar, January–March 1707/8; Stack MSS lj: Historical Relation, fols. 40–44; Abraham Whitrow, *A Prophetical Warning . . . to the People of Enfield. Feb. 22, 1707/8* [broadside] (London? 1707/8); *Collection of Prophetical Warnings*, pp. 147, 150; [Claude Groteste de la Mothe], *Examen du théâtre sacré des Cévennes* (London, 1708), pp. i–ii.

45. Calamy, *An Historical Account of My Own Life*, 1:99; Sir Richard Bulkeley, *Preface to the Reader of Warnings of the Eternal Spirit, Spoken by the Mouth of the Servant of God, Abraham Whitrow* (London, 1709), pp. 68–69. Lacy protested, "I am utterly ignorant that our Inspiration ever gave an order, to those who were pleased to hear us, that they should quit the sacred Ordinances and regular Ministry; on the contrary, it has acknowledged both. And I am very confident, most of our Followers have frequented those several forms of Congregations, to which their Inclinations before used to lead them" (*Relation of Dealings*, p. 17).

selves from James Jackson, whose vision Lacy had miraculously restored.[46]

There were both prophetic and political tensions in London in the early spring of 1708. At the end of March, the Stuart Pretender to the English throne, James Francis Edward, Prince of Wales and son of James II, was sailing to Scotland with French troops, and there were signs of panic in London, though the invasion was pitifully unsuccessful. Thunder crashed over the city, and two French Prophets predicted that fire and brimstone would pour down upon the wicked on March 25. Followers also expected a famine.[47]

When no famine came, when no fire and brimstone fell, followers found logic and prophets found inspirations that might both explain unconfirmed prediction and comfort the group in its confusion. If Dr. Emes failed to rise from the dead, it would be a sign not of the followers' delusion but of the unfaithfulness of the times, of a world not yet sufficiently prepared to appreciate such a miracle.[48]

Although contemporary satirists had Dr. Emes rising from his grave to address the multitudes gathered to await the miracle, the only fact in their May 25 fiction was the size of the crowd. One contemporary estimated that twenty thousand people milled about Emes's grave that Whit-Tuesday (while the major English prophets spent the day safely in the country outside London).[49] The possibility of mob action from a carefree holiday crowd of mixed character and generally low social status inspired political comment; one satire insinuated that the hullabaloo of the resurrection served the

46. James Jackson, *An Appeal to Country Friends* (London, 1708), pp. 4–7; Fatio Calendar, February 25, 1708; Friends' House Library (London), "Dictionary of Quaker Biography" (typescript), entry "James Jackson." See also William Beck and T. Frederick Ball, *The London Friends' Meetings* (London, 1869), p. 253; Henry Pickworth, *A Charge of Error* (London, 1716).

47. W. A. Speck, "Conflict in Society," in *Britain after the Glorious Revolution 1689–1715*, ed. Geoffrey Holmes (1970), p. 151; Fatio Calendar, March 18?, 1708; Samuel Keimer, *Brand pluck'd from the Burning* (London, 1718), pp. 28–31, 108.

48. See, e.g., *Collection of Prophetical Warnings*, pp. 2–3, 78–80, 103; Calamy, *An Historical Account of My Own Life*, 1:103–5; Bodleian Library (Oxford), Rawlinson MSS D.1152, fol. 115.

49. Fatio Calendar, May 25, 1708; Archives des Affaires Etrangères (Paris), Correspondance Politique, Angleterre, vol. 224, fol. 248 (letter from Abbé François Gaultier); *Flying Post*, no. 2040, May 25–27, 1708; Luttrell, *Brief Relation*, 6:307; "Dr. Emes's rising Speech" (written by Kingston), in Kingston, *Enthusiastick Impostors*, 2:141–42; *The French Prophet's Resurrection With His SPEECH to the Multitude that behold the Miracle* [broadside] (London, 1708).

interests of an evil party which intended to goad the people into an assault upon city and court.[50]

The French Prophets on May 26 were unrepentant and refused to accept the failure of the prediction as a sign that their inspired men, women, and children were guided by false spirits. Their numbers continued to increase, calling for an explanation that was not easily forthcoming: "And is it not an Amazing Consideration, that after such unquestionable demonstration of these Men's enthusiastical Blindness, or worse, that when their utmost expectation has failed them, and they have not the least hope of effecting what they had so often and so confidently promised, they should not yet be put to silence?"[51] The problems critics faced in their explanations for the behavior of the French Prophets had to do not only with physical actions but also with strength of belief, or, as Daniel Defoe wrote in surprise in June, the "Prevalency of this new Delusion."[52]

During the latter half of 1708, the French Prophets took stock of themselves, named each other into tribes, attempted to reconcile differences between French and English believers, expelled dissi-dent prophets, and celebrated a Great Jubilee. I too shall take stock of them at this point, for after a November armed battle between believers and hostile onlookers in Hackney Marsh just north of London,[53] the public gradually lost sight of the French Prophets, and the number of controversial works sharply decreased. In a sense the group retreated—into more private meetings; in a sense the group redirected its efforts—to missions to more distant places; and in a sense the group became more self-consciously reflective, examining standards for true inspiration.

At the end of 1708, there were four hundred French Prophets in London and environs, with twice as many English believers as

50. *A Letter from Dr. Emes to the MOB, Assembled at His Grave* (London, 1708), p. 4. The political overtones were partly the product of the change in the English ministry which had been going on since February; by November, the Whig Junto con-trolled Parliament, and serious party splits over the continental war made themselves manifest. See Keith Feiling, *A History of the Tory Party 1640–1714* (Oxford, 1924), pp. 393 ff.; Geoffrey Holmes, *British Politics in the Age of Anne* (London and New York, 1967), pp. 210–16.

51. Nathaniel Spinckes, *The New Pretenders to Prophecy Examined* (London, 1709), p. 430.

52. Daniel Defoe, *Review of the State of the English Nation*, vol. 5, no. 33 (June 12, 1708), p. 131.

53. Kingston, *Enthusiastick Impostors*, 2:168; *Post Boy*, no. 2111, November 23–25, 1708; Fatio Calendar, October 7–14, 1708; Archives des Affaires Etrangères (Paris), Corr. Politique, Angleterre, vol. 225, fols. 208–208v.

Huguenot, and twenty-two English prophets compared to fifteen Huguenot prophets. Beyond the significant English constituency of the group, what drew comment from critics was the age and sex of the inspired. They were on average under thirty years of age when they began to prophesy, and 40 per cent of them had become inspired before age twenty. In addition, there had come to be more female than male prophets, though inspired males still dominated the group socially. The average follower was about ten years older than the average prophet, and sex ratio in the entire group was imbalanced only slightly in favor of males, so the inspired could be distinguished from the uninspired by age, often by sex, and sometimes by social background as well as by physical action and speech. With the exceptions of John Lacy, John Potter, and Thomas Dutton, the prophets were noticeably younger and less well bred than the scribes who accompanied them. In comparison to Fatio, Bulkeley, Misson, Portales, and the other scribes, among whom were few young men and scarcely a woman, the number of young women and men who claimed to speak the Holy Word might be especially impressive.

So this was how the critics knew the French Prophets: as a religious group stimulated by Camisard *inspirés* but become predominantly English; as men and women who accepted divine inspiration from writhing or actively mimetic young people; as steadfast believers despite shoddy, transparent attempts at miracle and compromised predictions; as a ragtag assortment of Christian seekers with no distinct doctrine but the confidence that the millennium was (with no given date) at hand; as a confusingly diverse social group composed of a baronet, reputable gentlemen, physicians, merchants, artisans, shopkeepers, pie-vendors, laborers, and refugees without work or money. The critics would know little if anything about the French Prophets in later years— how they attracted a circle of Scottish quietists; how they made important contacts with continental pietists and encouraged communities of inspired separatists and mystics in Germany and Switzerland; how they in turn were influenced by Philadelphian and quietist forms; how they suffered a period of dissension between prophets and between French and English believers; how in the 1730s they experienced a renewal in the syncretic prophecies and leadership of a woman, Hannah Wharton; how, after brief successes among London Moravians and early Methodists, they again became silent; how at last the Shakers of Manchester claimed to have derived their illumination from the remnants of the French Prophets.[54] The future of the French Prophets did interest the opposition, but they paid less attention to the trends and changes within the religious group than to the spectre of the social disruption that would ensue if Camisard values became operative in English society.

The agitations and warnings of the prophets were unsettling enough in London's world of organized churches, registered meetinghouses, sedate ceremony, and academic sermons. Yet to account for the wide range of reactions against the French Prophets, one must consider as well the specific theological milieu into which had come Fage, Cavalier, and Marion—all three under the age of thirty, all veterans of a war fought not with printer's ink but with old muskets and with bullets fashioned from the lead of melted-down Catholic crucifixes. To the realm of pamphlet and pulpit I turn now as final preface.

THE MOVEMENT FOR SPIRITUAL REFORM

Although jeremiads about the decline of piety were current throughout the seventeenth century, as each Protestant faction applied its own favorite criteria of Christian behavior, after 1689 Protestants of all kinds had come to agree that theirs was peculiarly an age of irreligion. "How much is the World and many the highest Pretenders to Religion in it, alienated and changed from True Religion, and the Scope and Design thereof, in its primitive Purity and Plainness?" lamented that "Deist turned Christian" Thomas Emes in 1698.[55] The general sense of decline was in one regard a slightly delayed reaction to the supposed immorality of the Restoration period, its profane theater, its libertine court, its all-too-Catholic monarchs Charles II and James II.[56] In another regard, it was an overreaction to the influential principles of deism.

54. On the Scottish quietists, see George D. Henderson, ed., *Mystics of the North-East* (Aberdeen, 1934); on the Shakers, see Edward Deming Andrews and Faith Andrews, *The People Called Shakers*, new enlarged ed. (New York, 1963 [1953]).

55. Thomas Emes, *The Atheist turned Deist, and the Deist turned Christian; or, the Reasonableness and Union of Natural, and the True Christian Religion* (1698), p. 185.

56. See David Foxon, *Libertine Literature in England 1660–1747* (New Hyde Park, 1965) but compare Peter Laslett and Karla Oosterveen, "Long-term Trends in Bastardy in England," *Population Studies* 27 (1973):255–86.

Deism was itself a movement to restore the possibility of belief in an era that witnessed profound challenges to the Christian faith. Biblical scholars (led by the Frenchman Richard Simon) were uncovering the numerous mistranslations and mistranscriptions from original Greek and Aramaic Scriptures. Science, under the sway of Newtonian mechanics, seemed to reveal the natural laws by which, without mystery or miracle, the universe was regulated. People had new respect for the wisdom of the East, the Turkish philosopher and the Chinese sage who lived moral lives without the aid of Christianity.[57]

Deists responded to these challenges by advocating the primitive plainness of religion itself. Accepting the probability that Scripture accounts were historically unreliable, accepting too the assumptions of experimental science about the natural order of the world, the deists proposed to measure all revelations, natural or divine, by the inch-marks of reason. "For as 'tis by reason we arrive at the certainty of God's own existence," wrote John Toland in his famous deist manifesto, *Christianity not Mysterious* (1696), "so we cannot otherwise discern his revelations but by their conformity with our natural notices of him." Since, as commonly understood, the gifts of miracle and prophecy had ceased after apostolic times, good people, Christians or not, must conduct themselves in accordance with the moral principles that biblical miracle and prophecy had simply highlighted.[58]

Resort to reason, the universal human faculty, could reawaken popular religion. True Christianity—no mirage of supernatural events—was well within the scope of the poor and the illiterate, for, as Toland wrote, "the uncorrupted doctrines of Christianity are not above their reach or comprehension, but the gibberish of your divinity schools they understand not." Each person, according to the deists, had something within that could enable an appreciation of religion, if only human beings were not led astray into thickets of wonder stories, meaningless ceremony, and theological wrangling.

57. Frank E. Manuel, *The Eighteenth Century Confronts the Gods* (Cambridge, Mass., 1959); Paul Hazard, *The European Mind: The Critical Years (1680–1715)*, trans. J. Lewis May (New Haven, 1953).

58. John Toland, *Christianity not Mysterious* (1696), pp. 36, 153–73; Roger Lee Emerson, "English Deism 1670–1755: An Enlightenment Challenge to Orthodoxy" (Ph.D. diss., Brandeis University, 1962), esp. pp. 37, 43; Ernest C. Mossner, *Bishop Butler and the Age of Reason* (New York, 1936), p. 53.

Religion, at its root, was the human capacity to admire and imitate good behavior.[59]

Churchmen and Nonconformists alike took offense at this approach to the renewal of religion, for it exalted human reason to the detriment of Scripture and church order. Indeed, deists seemed to some to imply that Christian institutions and hierarchy had merely a social value. To others, the deist interpretation of the Bible verged upon heresy. Detractors associated deism with one of two heresies: Arianism, which denied Jesus' full divinity, and Socinianism, which disregarded the authority of Scripture and completely denied the divinity of Jesus. The similarity among deists, atheists, Arians, and Socinians, in the opinion of the orthodox, lay in their simplistic desire to avoid the incomprehensible.[60]

Replying to John Toland, Peter Browne asked whether "there be not some things in the Gospel concerning which we are bound to believe that there is much more in them than we are now able to comprehend." The standard orthodox answer to deism was that human reason was too feeble to master all revelation, that true Christianity was not as easily or as commonly recognized as deists hoped.[61] Finding people swamped by the "mysteries" of Christianity, deists wished to reconstruct the foundations for good behavior. The opponents found virtue and, indeed, moral lessons in the occasional obscurity of a scriptural passage.

Those who rejected deist strategy and philosophy had still to deal with the decadence they saw mirrored in the deists' very critique of revealed religion. They opted for societies for religious reform. These societies directed all effort toward visible, measurable achievement. Unlike the deist orientation to subtle and individual change, the orthodox approach was broadly social and destined to give the churches prominence. In an era when the relationship between church and state was much debated, when the sermons of

59. Toland, *Christianity not Mysterious*, p. 147; Manuel, *Eighteenth Century Confronts the Gods*, pp. 59, 61.

60. Roland N. Stromberg, *Religious Liberalism in Eighteenth-Century England* (London, 1954), pp. 9–10, 34, 50; Walker, *Decline of Hell*, pp. 9, 16, 26; Rosalie L. Colie, "Spinoza and the Early English Deists," *Journal of the History of Ideas* 20 (1959):23–46; John Redwood, *Reason, Ridicule and Religion: The Age of Enlightenment in England 1660–1750* (Cambridge, Mass., 1976), pp. 156–213.

61. Peter Browne, *A Letter in Answer to a Book entitled Christianity not Mysterious* (Dublin, 1697), excerpted in E. Graham Waring, ed., *Deism and Natural Religion: A Source Book* (New York, 1967), p. 28; Stromberg, *Religious Liberalism*, pp. 22, 69. Cf. Redwood, *Reason, Ridicule and Religion*, pp. 214–23.

the Reverend Dr. Henry Sacheverell on that subject in 1709 could arouse popular as well as legislative passions, the Church as an institution was not far from the minds of the devout.[62] In an era when the officers of city government were required to attend Anglican communion whether or not they conformed to Anglican doctrine, the outward forms of religious worship could not be ignored, and the public controversy and political haggling over the "occasional conformity" of dissenting magistrates was proof of the importance attributed to visible religious activity.

The orthodox initiated their societies in the belief that the declining piety so evident to them was the result of ignorance of God's Word; sure that prolonged exposure to Scripture could remedy much, they sought to spread knowledge of Scripture to the most humble. But they had hopes, too, of returning to the harmonious society and spirit of the early Christians. John Lacy, member of the Societies for the Reformation of Manners, founded in 1691, wrote: "In the Primitive Ages of Christianity they say, there was, under Variety of Administrations, an illustrious Union of Affections; Light and Love were not so disjoined; Humility made them willing to stoop mutually to one another; but is the Report hereof to be disowned, or has that one, Uniting, Spirit, the Coelestial Dove, withdrawn from this Relapsed and Apostate World."[63] In "this Relapsed and Apostate World," the Societies for the Reformation of Manners managed to shut down five hundred houses of ill fame, though early hampered by the overzealous activities of the reformer Sir Richard Bulkeley. The Society for Promoting Christian Knowledge (founded 1696) printed and distributed thousands of Bibles and worked closely with the Society for the Propagation of the Gospel in Foreign Parts (founded 1701) to extend Christian brotherhood and the apostolic spirit to American Indians.[64] These were public, social, and highly apparent actions. Results might be plotted in terms of church attendance, numbers of Bibles in the

62. See Geoffrey Holmes, "The Sacheverell Riots: The Crowd and the Church in Early Eighteenth-Century London," *Past and Present* 72 (1976):55–85.
63. John Lacy, *A Letter to Sir H. Mackworth, Concerning His Treatise About the Late Occasional Bill*, 2d ed.? (London, 1704), p. 12. Lacy was defending the right of Dissenters to establish nominal conformity with the Anglican church by attending church services occasionally.
64. Bahlmann, *The Moral Revolution of 1688*, pp. 19–21, on Bulkeley; Christopher Hill, "Propagating the Gospel," in *Historical Essays 1600–1750 Presented to David Ogg*, ed. H. E. Bell and R. L. Ollard (London, 1963), pp. 35–59; W. K. Lowther Clark, *A History of the S.P.C.K.* (London, 1959).

poorest houses, numbers of converts, the state of sexual morality as proven by the absence of prostitutes. Orthodox reform was based upon a faith that outward forms would affect the inner person; the deists, less attached to institutions, pursued only the bones and not the tissue of Christianity.

The Camisard prophets entered an England in which the illiterate had sympathies for the victims of Catholic persecution but suspicions of Frenchmen; in which the literate, aware of controversy over prophecy and miracles, reason and revelation, had not forsworn the value of either but acknowledged the importance of a vital national church; and in which the campaigning reformers deplored the morality of the age and wished to renew religion through Scripture. These attitudes could swing English Protestants now near to, now far from the millenarianism of the *inspirés*. In the face of new prophecy, opponents of deism could choose to exalt the prophets as evidence of the primacy of revelation or could determine to defend Christianity from those who, like deists, made a mockery of original revelation. The common people might regard the new prophets as Protestant guerillas and survivors of Catholic violence, or as Frenchmen, likely Jesuit plotters in a well-designed intrigue against church and queen. Reformers might acclaim the prophets' jeremiads against English religious "deadness" as appropriate evangelism for revival, or as exaggerated sermons undermining the credibility of true evangelical endeavors. Thomas Emes, John Lacy, and Sir Richard Bulkeley believed the new prophets to be possessed of the genuine apostolic spirit; many other reformers decided that the prophets subverted Christian piety.

Whatever the social or theological context, there were many possible responses to the French Prophets. Their special notoriety was due in good measure to the fact that their claims to prophecy and miracle put them in the center of a heated controversy over reason and revelation. While the French Prophets played out their drama in a popular theater which others had built, their opponents refined and articulated a theory of human behavior.

2. The Critique

UNBELIEVERS described the French Prophets variously as possessed, deluded, deceived, insane, and enthusiastic. These descriptions had much in common. They were grounded in similar philosophical and social assumptions. Each of them involved a different metaphor (devil, disease, or contagion) to express fundamentally the same understanding of human behavior.

The French Prophets appeared in England at a time when deist battled Anglican, High Churchman staved off Latitudinarian, particular Baptist expelled general Baptist, and everyone deplored faction. All parties to religious controversy and all manner of scientists attacked the French Prophets. A critic's choice of terms for attack reflected his religious party and scientific theories, but the consensus of the attack was more remarkable than the diversity of terms.

What critics were agreed upon was the sinuous relationship of soul to body, the ability of mental or emotional states to affect flesh and blood. Although each had a favorite metaphor by which to explain the mechanics of the relationship, all critics regarded the actions and beliefs of the French Prophets as symptoms of something abnormal in the soul-body alliance. Contemporary medical knowledge supplied the paradigms for such a view and often the very language for its expression.

ANIMAL SPIRITS

In the late seventeenth century and early eighteenth century, medical theory about physical disturbance relied heavily upon the notion of animal spirits. These were the mysterious but crucial agents by which the soul could affect the body. The *British Apollo*, a newspaper of "Curious Amusements for the Ingenious," received this question from a correspondent in 1708: "I observe you solve a great many Questions by the Operation of the Animal Spirits, therefore beg of you to tell me what those Animal Spirits are?" The *British Apollo* answered in as straightforward and precise a fashion as one was likely to find anywhere: "The Animal Spirits are Particles of the Blood so exceedingly Rarified and by Mutual Collision so particularly Configurated, as to be Capable of a Swifter Motion, and of a free Passage through such Parts of the Body as are Impervious to the other Particles of the Blood."[1] Henry Nicholson, an apostate French Prophet, writing *A Brief Treatise of the Anatomy of Humane Bodies* (1709), located the operation of animal spirits in the nerve canals. Following the Cartesian dogma that there is no vacuum in nature, Nicholson claimed that the hollow tubes of nerves "must (for all Cavity, or Space, will draw Substance to fill it, 'tis impossible it should be even apprehended otherwise) draw from the Blood a fluid Juice of equal Gravity and Substance with the Air, or less and more minute than Air. This Juice, whatsoever it be, is what we may apprehend under the Name and Notion of the Animal Spirit."[2] The association of animal spirits with nerve fluids was as common as the acknowledgment that no one knew much more about them. In modern terms, "animal spirits" was the label for electrochemical nerve impulses, still imperfectly understood.[3]

Imponderable, invisible, "rarified" fluid matter had been recalled into being by seventeenth-century scientists. Cartesian and then Newtonian postulates demanded a medium by which physical forces could be translated through distances. In Descartes' full world of infinitely divisible particles moving in vortices, the guarantor of physical contact between all particles in the *plenum* was a first kind of matter so small that it fitted snugly in the spaces between the particles of the *matière subtile*, aether. Newton, contemplating a

    1. *British Apollo*, vol. 1, no. 37 (June 16–18, 1708).
    2. Page 33. Cf. Edwin Clarke, "The Doctrine of the Hollow Nerve in the Seventeenth and Eighteenth Centuries," in *Medicine, Science and Culture*, ed. Lloyd G. Stevenson and Robert P. Multhauf (Baltimore, 1968), pp. 123–42; Arthur O. Lovejoy, *The Great Chain of Being* (Cambridge, Mass., 1964 [1936]), pp. 181–82.
    3. See Russell Brain, "The Concept of Hysteria in the Time of William Harvey," *Proceedings of the Royal Society of Medicine* 56 (April 1963):322.

world of great open spaces and small hard particles, began with and—after a decade of hesitations—returned to the premise that the void itself is occupied by a fine, subtle matter known as aether. For both men, the problem of physical forces acting at a distance was solved by recourse to something invisible, fluid, and corporeal. For Descartes, the existence of the first kind of matter entirely eliminated the problem of action at a distance. For Newton and many of his associates (Boyle being more reticent than the others) the existence of aether as a communicating medium made sense of gravitational forces acting over long distances throughout the universe.[4]

Both men also recognized that the mechanisms they proposed for the operation of physical forces had physiological analogues. For Descartes, the first kind of matter in the human system was the animal spirits, the medium by which the thinking soul, *l'âme raisonable*, made contact with the active body. The soul communicated with the pineal gland, and the pineal gland affected the animal spirits, which in turn coursed through the nerves and brought the soul's movements to the vital spirits in the muscles. For Newton, the "common aether" whose existence simplified the explanation of optical phenomena had its counterpart in the "aethereal animal spirit" of the human body. The soul directed the animal spirits through the nerves and so moved the muscles.[5]

4. Max Jammer, *Concepts of Force: A Study in the Foundations of Dynamics* (Cambridge, Mass., 1957), pp. 103, 115, 134–39; Marie Boas, *Robert Boyle and Seventeenth-Century Chemistry* (Cambridge, 1958), pp. 80–81; Mary B. Hesse, *Forces and Fields: The Concept of Action at a Distance in the History of Physics* (London and New York, 1961), pp. 103–11, 115–19; J. E. McGuire, "Force, Active Principles, and Newton's Invisible Realm," *Ambix* 15 (1968):154–208; Arnold Thackray, *Atoms and Powers: An Essay on Newtonian Matter-Theory and the Development of Chemistry* (Cambridge, Mass., 1970), pp. 40, 129–30; Richard S. Westfall, *Force in Newton's Physics: The Science of Dynamics in the Seventeenth Century* (London and New York, 1971), pp. 364–75, 391–410; P. M. Heimann, "'Nature is a perpetual worker': Newton's Aether and Eighteenth-Century Natural Philosophy," *Ambix* 20 (1973):1–25. See also chap. 3, note 4.

5. E. Bastholm, *The History of Muscle Physiology from the Natural Philosophers to Albrecht von Haller*, Acta Historica Scientiarum Naturalium et Medicinalium, no. 7 (Copenhagen, 1950), pp. 135–41, 190, 216–17; I. Bernard Cohen and Robert E. Schofield, eds., "Newton's Second Paper on Light and Colours (1675)," in *Isaac Newton's Papers and Letters On Natural Philosophy and related documents* (Cambridge, Mass., 1958), pp. 179–84. Contrast William Coleman, "Mechanical Philosophy and the Hypothetical Physiology," in *The "Annus Mirabilis" of Sir Isaac Newton 1666–1966*, ed. R. Palter (Cambridge, Mass., 1970), pp. 322–32. See also

The physics and physiology of aether and animal spirits were developed in a consciously theological context. The issue was this: how does God act in the physical world? With Aristotelian conviction, Descartes entirely divorced spiritual from physical forces, yet he maintained that there was constant dialogue between thinking soul and material body. The dialogue was mediated by "a very fine wind or rather a very lively and very pure flame," those animal spirits whose composition was so mysterious as to lead to serious dilemmas about the distinction between human beings and machines. How *did* humans as physical beings participate in the spiritual? Newton suggested that forces in the natural world were correspondent to divine activity; aether in the universe, like aethereal animal spirits in the body, was the medium by which spiritual forces entered the human realm.[6]

In order to assess the inspirations and convulsions of the French Prophets, critics tended to resort to theories about physiological or emotional forces which had immediate parallels in contemporary theories about physical forces. Just as small and seemingly weightless particles were integral to the demonstration of hypotheses about the mechanical translation of physical forces, so they were integral to the understanding of religious behavior which implied direct true communication between the spiritual and the physical. Animal spirits penetrated the entire body, from outermost limbs to innermost organs, from heart to head. In the brain, where some physicians located the seat of the soul, animal spirits made their contact with the spiritual realm. Mind and emotion, composites of the soul,

---

D. M. Needham, *Machina Carnis; the Biochemistry of Muscular Contraction in its Historical Development* (Cambridge, 1971); G. S. Rousseau, "Science and the Discovery of the Imagination in Enlightened England," *Eighteenth-Century Studies* 3 (Fall 1969): 108–35. I have not seen T. M. Brown, "The Mechanical Philosophy and the 'Animal Oeconomy'; a Study in the Development of English Physiology in the Seventeenth and Early Eighteenth Century" (Ph.D. diss., Princeton University, 1968).

6. Bastholm, *History of Muscle Physiology*, p. 136; Albert G. A. Balz, "Cartesian Doctrine and the Animal Soul," in his *Cartesian Studies* (New York, 1951), pp. 106–57; Aram Vartanian, ed., *La Mettrie's L'Homme Machine: A Study in the Origins of an Idea* (Princeton, 1960), p. 238n et passim; Heikki Kirkinen, *Les origines de la conception moderne de l'homme machine*, in Annales Academiae Scientarum Fennicae, ser. B, vol. 122 (Helsingfors, 1961), pp. 69–73, 124, 282; McGuire, "Force, Active Principles, and Newton's Invisible Realm," pp. 156–64, 193–206; Hélène Metzger, *Attraction universelle et religion naturelle chez quelques commentateurs anglais de Newton* (Paris, 1938), pp. 55–78; Alexandre Koyré, *From the Closed World to the Infinite Universe* (Baltimore, 1957), pp. 206–20.

affected the body through the sensitive medium of animal spirits. The condition of the animal spirits mirrored the changing states of the soul, so that "When the Mind is disturbed by some grievous accident, the animal Spirits run into disorderly motions."[7]

Accepting the principle of inertia on the physiological level, critics assumed that under normal circumstances the animal spirits move steadily through the body, unimpeded and unaccelerated. The test of health was the capacity of the animal spirits to return quickly to their original motion after each sensible shock from the environment. Physicians credited the irregular motion of the animal spirits with the power to cause a variety of widely diagnosed illnesses: hysteria, the vapors, madness, hypochondria. These illnesses had primary mental as well as physical symptoms and exemplified the interplay of soul and body, which so complemented one another that "There is no action of the Mind that does not have a correspondent one in the Body; nor no motion of the Body that does not produce a suitable affection in the Mind."[8] If animal spirits rushed about violently, they caused convulsions. If they were inhibited from free flow by "Black Vapours" clogging the nerve vessels, that made for madness. If they ran "confusedly and at random into the common Sensory," delirium occurred.[9] Popular nostrums for the palsy and pills for head and brain were advertised with promises of restoring natural vigor to the animal spirits, dissolving obstructions to their free passage.

The process threatened circularity: the soul sent the animal spirits whirling and they in turn upset the body and the soul. Physicians

7. Humphrey Sydenham, *Dr. Sydenham's Compleat Method of Curing Almost All Diseases*, 3d ed. (London, 1697), p. 6. Cf. Kenneth Dewhurst, *Dr. Thomas Sydenham (1624–1689)* (Berkeley and Los Angeles, 1966), p. 174.

8. John Trenchard, *The Natural History of Enthusiasm* (London, 1709), pp. 17–18, cited by Manuel, *The Eighteenth Century Confronts the Gods*, p. 77. Cf. the review of Friedrich Hoffman's *Dissertationes Physico-Medicae* (Leiden, 1708), in *The History of the Works of the Learned*, 10:4 (1708).

9. Sydenham, *Compleat Method*, p. 158; Thomas Willis, *The London Practice of Physick* (London, 1685), p. 449; Thomas Fallowes, *The Best Method for the Care of Lunatics* (London, 1705), p. 10; James Harvey, *Praesagium Medicum* (London, 1706), p. 4. On iatromechanics and vitalist and animist medical theory, see Julian Jaynes, "The Problem of Animate Motion in the Seventeenth Century," *Journal of the History of Ideas* 31 (1970):219–34; Christopher Hill, *Change and Continuity in in Seventeenth-Century England* (London, 1974), pp. 175–76; Lester S. King, "Rationalism in Early Eighteenth Century Medicine," *Journal of the History of Medicine* 18 (1963):257–71; idem, "Stahl and Hoffman: A Study in Eighteenth Century Animism," *Journal of the History of Medicine* 19 (1964):118–30.

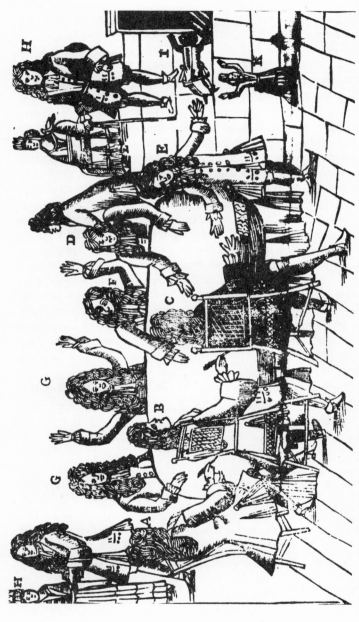

A Meeting of the French Prophets, depicted in *The English and French Prophets Mad or Bewitcht, At their Assemblies in Baldwins Gardens* (1707). A. French Prophet stamping. B. Benjamin Jackson, scribe. C. Another scribe. D. Sir Richard Bulkeley. E. Dutton the lawyer. F. Lacy shaking his head. G. Converts not yet come to the full Spirit of Prophecy. H. Spectators. I. Little boy being disturbed, cursing the people. K. Female prophet of seven years of age. L. Betty Gray with a dove which flew upon her shoulder.

hoped to arrest the spiraling progress of mind-related illnesses by interrupting, often with a heavy hand, at some critical point: by bleeding to remove obstacles, by prescription of metal-based medicines (mercury, zinc, or steel compounds) to restore strength sympathetically. Physicians sought to put the body and soul once again into their primitive harmony by the only means at their disposal, action upon the physical intermediary, animal spirits. The French Prophet Dr. Timothy Byfield wrote, "I'll endeavour to direct [the Soul] into an harmonious Union with the Body, by the help of the Spirit, which is a small portion of the purest Air, a middle Nature, betwixt the Body and Soul; light and invisible, tempered with Fire, Volatile and a most pure Substance, begetting Vital Spirits."[10] The sensitivity of pure animal spirits explained how the soul communicated with the body and how delicate was the balance between them. The links among brain, nerves, and musculature were so constant and direct that any irritant which entered the system, physical or spiritual, would disturb all elements.

Unlike physicians, the inspired among the French Prophets appeared to welcome disturbance. In fact, they diagnosed their agitations as symptoms of a disease in which the intermediary was the Holy Spirit, close correlate to animal spirits. In narratives of their experiences, the inspired described in almost clinical detail the process by which the Spirit acted upon their bodies. It entered the body at points traditionally thought most congenial to a mediating relationship with the soul: the mouth and lungs, the heart, the head. Prophets' accounts of the symptoms associated with inspiration made the Holy Spirit seem as much a physical substance as were the volatile and pure-as-air animal spirits. Elie Marion said, "I perceived on a sudden a great Burning round my Heart, that spread after over all my Body; I was also a little oppressed at the Lungs, that made me fetch deep Sighs, but I suppressed them, what I could; some Moments after, an irresistible Force prevailed over me altogether, which made me cry out with Interruptions of Gulping like a Hiccup, and my Eyes poured out a Flood of Tears." Jean Cavalier was even more specific: "there seemed a beating as of a hammer in my Breast,which kindled a Flame that took me, and dispersed over all my Veins, this put me into a sort of leaping, which flung me

10. Timothy Byfield, *Horae Subsecivae: Or, Some Long-Vacation Hours Redeemed* (London, 1695), p. 2. Cf. L. J. Rather, *Mind and Body in Eighteenth Century Medicine* (London, 1965), pp. 1–15.

down; I rose again without any harm, and as my Heart was lifted up to God with unutterable fervor, I was struck a second time, and my Flame increased; my Prayers grew also more ardent, speaking and breathing with mighty Groans; soon after, a third Blow took me on the Breast, and set me all in a Fire; some moments of respite intervened, and then followed on a sudden violent Agitations of the Head and Body, and like unto those I have had since."[11] Among the English prophets, there were similar descriptions. John Lacy believed that the Holy Spirit and animal spirits cooperated. While meditating in his prayer closet, Lacy had more than twenty times "found something dart or strike upon my Forehead represented to the Intellect (without any visible Appearance) like a Flash of Fire, which gave a sudden turn to the animal Spirits, and from the Head perceptibly dispersed itself all over my Body; which conveyed therewith into my Soul, a referential Awe, Suavity, and Joy inexpressible, purely Divine."[12] Here too was circularity, but for the French Prophets this was wonderful and desirable, a spiraling toward God. One disposed the soul (intellect and emotions) to receive the Spirit, which, when it arrived, so moved the animal spirits that the soul was further disposed to receive divine impressions. Shivering, gasping, and leaping were visible parallels to the invisible process whereby soul and body were brought into perfect harmony.

The prophets stressed the irresistible nature of the Holy Spirit and its physical effects. They learned to recognize their agitations as harbingers of inspiration, and they believed these motions to be so unnatural that they "did afford a Moral Assurance to all Observers, that he [the prophet] neither spake, or acted by his own Will, as other Men."[13] Durand Fage, musing upon his inspirations and those of others, insisted that "every individual Person is different in his Agitations, according to the Circumstance and Nature of those things he is to pronounce; but all those who speak by Inspiration have this in common, which is (as I have already observed) that the Words are formed in their Mouths, without any Purpose or Direction on their Parts; in like Manner, is their Body moved by an

11. *A Cry from the Desart* (London, 1707), pp. 41, 84–85. This is the English translation of Misson, *Le théâtre sacré des Cévennes.*
12. John Lacy, *A Letter to the Reverend Dr. Josiah Woodward* (1708), p. 18. This and all subsequently cited controversial works by French Prophets and opponents have London as their place of publication unless otherwise noted.
13. John Lacy, *The General Delusion of Christians* (1713), p. 229.

overriding influence, unto the Power of which their several Members are yielded up."[14] Fage was saying two things: agitations were not just storm warnings for spoken prophecy but a physical shorthand of the prophecy itself; since agitations were another vehicle of divine speech, both physical and spoken prophecy were involuntary. Involuntary action guaranteed the purity of the divine message, for then there would be no human meddling with or garbling of meaning. Many prophets, as evidence of the "overriding influence," claimed that they could not remember what they had said under ecstasy. All of them noted that their lives had been significantly altered by their prophetic experiences.[15] Agitations thus symbolized a changed moral state as well as a kind of prophetic act: they demonstrated time and again the terrible struggle human beings must undergo to arrive at spiritual conversion. Without their succumbing to the Holy Spirit, neither prophecy nor conversion could take place. Respect for the overpowering Holy Spirit was a serious matter. "I have more than once, with the most awful Solemnity," wrote John Lacy, "declared and published in Print, that in the times of my Ecstasy, I am under the agency of another distinct Being." If the exact manner by which the Holy Spirit assumed this agency remained unknown, it was perhaps because "the manner of an immaterial Soul's Union with [the Body] for a Time affords yet Room, after the utmost Exertions of our natural Faculties, for a clearer Solution."[16] Thomas Dutton, another of the prophets, could warn those who lacked respect for the inspired, "Ye know not the Ways of God; Ye know not how your own Souls act upon your Bodies; much less are ye capable to know, the Ways of the Spirit of God."[17]

Whether the agent was the Spirit or animal spirits, literate people of the early eighteenth century shared the assumption that matter could be operated upon by invisible forces (passions, thought, the complex that was the soul). They believed that body and soul not only communed but interacted, and they highly valued the preservation of harmony between them. Like physicians, and unlike the French Prophets, critics could not accept agitations, physical or

14. *Cry from the Desart*, pp. 71–72.
15. Ibid., pp. 21, 85.
16. Lacy, *Letter to Woodward*, pp. 3–4, and *General Delusion*, p. 5. Cf. Lacy's *Relation of Dealings*, pp. 9–10.
17. Thomas Dutton, John Glover, and Guy Nutt, *Warnings of the Eternal Spirit, to the City of Edenburgh* (London, 1710), pp. 42–43.

social, as symbols of work toward that harmony. Accustomed to judging physically abnormal states as symptomatic of disease, and socially abnormal states as precursors of danger to the body politic, critics could not attribute agitations to some positive force. If the Holy Spirit entered one's body, it was sure to do so gently. True inspiration and true religion were in complete accord with and never overrode reason.[18]

In effect, prophet and skeptic were rendering divergent moral judgments on the same phenomena from almost the same viewpoint. Both understood that physical states mirrored moral condition. The French Prophets, whose faith extended to a belief that abnormal physical states were nonetheless moral, regarded agitations as signs of spiritual progress, proofs of inspiration, and figures of prophetic speech. Critics, more cautious, informed by the deist controversy or by the new science or private millennial schemes, had no such faith. The forces to which the prophets succumbed had consequently to be shown other than divine.

In one way or another, hostile descriptions of the French Prophets were founded upon a distrust of irresistible forces playing havoc with the soul-body relationship through their effect on an invisible mediating substance. Reinforced by theological arguments which denied the need for new prophets, critics regarded the inspired as all-too-willing victims of vague but tremendous and harmful forces. Between 1707 and 1710, ninety books,[19] pamphlets, and journal and newspaper articles were published against the French Prophets; most of them advanced theories about how human beings are over-powered by some element, natural or unnatural. A survey of these works sheds light not only on the contemporary reaction to an

18. Cf. George Keith, *The Magick of Quakerism* (1707), pp. 54, 83–84.

19. Books usually were printed in editions of 500 to 1,000, at an average price of 13 pence. The French Prophets considered publishing 800 copies of James Cuninghame's Tolbooth warnings but thought that too much, considering the hesitance of booksellers to handle French Prophet publications for fear of harassment. At least 1,450 copies were printed of Elie Marion's *Prophetical Warnings*. See C. John Sommerville, "Popular Religious Literature in England 1660–1711: A Content Analysis" (Ph.D. diss., University of Iowa, 1970), pp. 12, 37–41, which appears in much revised form in this monograph series as *Popular Religion in Restoration England* (Gainesville, 1977); idem, "On the Distribution of Religious and Occult Literature in Seventeenth-Century England," *The Library* 29 (1974):221–25; Mitchell Library (Glasgow), MSS Slaines Collection 562590, Correspondence between Thomas Dutton and James Cuninghame, 1709–40, letter of May 2, 1710; British Museum copy of Marion's *Prophetical Warnings*, notation (in the hand of Nicolas Fatio?) on page before title page.

aggressive millenarian group, but also on early eighteenth-century views of human behavior.

"THE SUBTILE EFFLUVIUM"

Eubulus, reviewing Sir Richard Bulkeley's comprehensive *Answer to Several Treatises* for the monthly *Censura Temporum*, had no space left to discuss Bulkeley's account of the miraculous acts of the French Prophets. He did however assure Sophronius that the account contained "only such Matters as are consistent with Hypocrisy, Delusion, good Guessing, subtle Scrutinies, underhand Intelligence, forelaid Contrivance and Artifice, the Warmth of a Delirious and Enthusiastic Imagination, or, at most, the Power and Activity of Evil Spirits, whose Agency, no doubt, must be necessary to the working of those Signs and Wonders, which, if it were possible, would deceive the very Elect."[20] Eubulus had listed the range of alternative explanations available to critics of the French Prophets: possession, delusion, deception or fraud, disease, enthusiasm. Like Eubulus, many critics availed themselves of several explanations at once, suggesting that a common thread ran through them all.

Those who stressed possession by the devil were definitely in the minority. Eubulus himself, with his temporizing "at most," had mentioned the devil as a last resort. As witchcraft accusations declined and the learned approached witchcraft and possession with skepticism, only the oldest opponent of the French Prophets, John Humfrey (1621–1719), could not "choose but suspect there is some Witchery among them, and they know it not."[21] Newspapers and Birmingham constables took solemnly the possibility of satanic

20. *Censura Temporum*, vol. 1, no. 4 (April 1708), p. 116. Cf. F.-Maximilien Misson, *Meslange de literature historique et critique* (1707), preface.

21. John Humfrey, *A Farther Account of our Late Prophets* (1708), pp. 14–15. He also may have been using the term *witchcraft* very loosely; see his *An Account of the French Prophets* (1708), p. 19. On Humfrey himself, see Douglas R. Lacey, *Dissent and Parliamentary Politics in England, 1661–1689: A Study in the Perpetuation and Tempering of Parliamentarianism* (New Brunswick, N.J., 1969), pp. 23–29, 56–68, 226–27. On the decline of witchcraft accusations, see K. V. Thomas, *Religion and the Decline of Magic* (New York, 1971), pp. 481–98; Alan Macfarlane, *Witchcraft in Tudor and Stuart England* (New York, 1970); H. R. Trevor-Roper, "The European Witch-craze of the Sixteenth and Seventeenth Centuries," in his *Religion, the Reformation, and Social Change, and Other Essays* (London, 1967), p. 97; W. B. Carnochan, "Witch-Hunting and Belief in 1751: The Case of Thomas Colley and Ruth Osborne," *Journal of Social History* 4 (1971):389–403.

agency among the prophets, but even they made no reference to witchcraft.[22] The possession hypothesis was favored by clergymen who wished to refute deist, Socinian, and atheist while they denounced false prophets. Humfrey, a Congregational minister, wrote with a touch of sadness, "One Observation I will make by the Way, that whether it be by a Good or Bad Spirit that these Men do act, yet so long as it is by any Spirit, it does serve to convince the Atheist and this Unbelieving Age of the Being of Invisible Things, and the Reasonableness of Religion."[23] Unwilling to reduce all events to natural causes, the clerics who felt threatened by the scientific predisposition, or who equated naturalism with materialism and skepticism, tried to show that no reasonable hypothesis answered so well the dilemmas posed by the new prophets as that of satanic agency. In answer to the earl of Shaftesbury's graceful but single-minded insistence that the French Prophets were subjects of enthusiastic "panic," two authors brought forward the possession hypothesis to assail deist and prophet simultaneously. One anonymous author made certain too that all were in accord on the soul-body relationship: "Though this *Daemoniacal* Enthusiasm may be as intelligible, I think, as any other kind, and I know 'tis every whit as easy to be understood, as the Actings of our *own* Spirits and Bodies upon each other; and though we have vast plenty of Proofs that there *hath* been such a thing, and *still* is, yet it is grown very Modish (however it comes to pass) to *seem* to disbelieve it."[24] The second author, Dr. Edward Fowler (1632–1714), latitudinarian Bishop of Gloucester, passionately interested in ghost stories and accounted a follower by the French Prophets themselves, could not see any natural explanation for their extraordinary physical movements. The prophets were, in his opinion in 1709, acted upon as they claimed to be, by a supernatural agent. The agent unfortunately resembled the devil and not the Holy Spirit.[25] Offspring Blackall, Bishop of Exeter, preaching before the Queen in 1707, was not

22. *The Observator*, August 6–9, 1707; Nathaniel Spinckes, *The New Pretenders to Prophecy Re-examined* (1710), app. 1, pp. 27–28.

23. Humfrey, *A Farther Account*, p. 16.

24. *Remarks on the Letter to a Lord concerning Enthusiasm* (1709), p. 68. On Shaftesbury, see below, pp. 53–54.

25. *Reflections Upon a Letter concerning Enthusiasm* (1709), pp. 3, 55–57, 63–64; *Dictionary of National Biography* 7:525 (on Fowler, b. 1632, second oldest of the critics). Fowler is named in one French Prophet membership list, B.P.U.G., MSS fr. 605, list with tribe markings.

impressed by the agitations of the French Prophets, for the devil "is able to do far greater things than any that as yet have been so much as reported to have been done by our New Prophets."[26]

Most critics, however, twenty or more years younger than Humfrey and Fowler, shied away from the possession hypothesis.[27] The shift toward a medical explanation or analogy was apparent in works that coupled possession with insanity. The Anglican minister Francis Hutchinson, who later diagnosed witchcraft symptoms as hysteria, thought that the behavior of the prophets under inspiration was particularly suspect: their "Whistling, Singing, Drumming, and Laughing" were the "usual Signs of Madness or Possession, but no ways agreeable to Divine Inspiration."[28] Benjamin Bayly, rector in Bristol and one of the youngest critics (1671–1720), believed that "had St. Paul appeared to the Nations to whom he preached like one of our *new Prophets, hiccuping, gulping, foaming, tumbling, whistling*, etc., he would have had little Attention or Regard paid him, he would have been thought a mad Man or Daemoniac instead of an Apostle."[29] This transition from evil spirits to animal spirits as explanation was facilitated by a popular intermediate hypothesis: delusion. When Birmingham followers renounced the dispensation, they confessed that their belief was all "a mere Delusion of the Devil."[30] Henry Nicholson, in the midst of his medical analysis, thought it probable that the "delusive Impressions" of his former companions were promoted by evil spirits.[31] The devil and his agents worked to prepare the way for delusion and to rope people into a delusive maze. This perspective on the devil's role was a comforting step away from the theological dilemma posed by satanic possession: why did God allow the devil to possess good people?[32]

26. Blackall, *The Way of Trying Prophets* (1707), p. 22.

27. See Appendix for profiles of the opponents. Note that the third oldest critic, Richard Kingston (born ca. 1635), wrote, "What can be said less, than that Men are possessed with a *Devil*, when they rave, fight, tear their own Flesh, beat their Heads Against a Wall, dash themselves against the Ground, foam at the Mouth, and are seized with all the frightful Symptoms of the *Demoniac* in the Gospel." *Enthusiastic Impostors No Divinely Inspired Prophets*, 2 parts (1707–9), 1:26.

28. Hutchinson, *A Short View of the Pretended Spirit of Prophecy* (1708), p. 35. Cf. Ilza Veith, *Hysteria: The History of a Disease* (Chicago, 1965), pp. 90–134.

29. Benjamin Bayly, *An Essay upon Inspiration*, 2d ed. (1708), p. 403.

30. G. P., *The Shortest Way with the French Prophets* (1708), p. 6; Spinckes, *Pretenders Re-examined*, app. 1, p. 29.

31. Henry Nicholson, *Falsehood of the New Prophets* (1708), p. 13.

32. For examples of doctrine on divine permission for possession, see Thomas

Delusion simply implied that the devil might be a predisposing factor, particularly in religious delusions which had such grave social consequences. George Hickes, Anglican High Churchman, born in 1642, wrote that the spirit of delusion in the French Prophets gave occasion to the "common Enemies of Revealed Religion, the *Atheists*, *Deists*, and *Sceptics*, to blaspheme God," as if all divine messengers had been of the same equivocal stature as these new self-proclaimed prophets.[33]

The difference between possession and delusion was the difference between exorcism and pity, and as one expressed pity, one adopted natural explanations. Daniel Defoe, "loth to offer any thing to these poor Deluded People, that is sharp or bitter," prayed that God might restore their judgment.[34] The anonymous author of *A Letter from Dr. Emes to the MOB*, regarding the prophets and their adherents as "Objects of Pity, not of Fury, tricked by the Devil and his Agents into unheard-of Delusions," thought too that they had "suffered Shipwrack of their Senses."[35] Interviewing a prophet, the latitudinarian minister Josiah Woodward extracted from her the confession that "she was drawn into a Snare, deluded, and utterly undone," and further, that "her Brains were turned in her Head, by being among them."[36]

However fanciful the metaphorical "shipwrack of the senses" or the "turned brain," these physical images verged on the medical. Delusion, like melancholy, came within the realm of both philosopher and physician. Under the rubric of distraction or distempered mind fell much behavior which, though admittedly mysterious, would no longer be attributed to demons. "It is to be remembered," wrote Benjamin Bayly, who did not utterly exclude all "Diabolic Assistance" yet stressed natural causes, "how little the Philosophy of the Mind is understood; and every sensible Man sees in Fact,

Morer, *Sermons on Several Occasions* (1708), p. 223; *An Appeal from the Prophets to their Prophecies* (1708), p. 15.

33. Hickes, *The Spirit of Enthusiasm Exorcised*, 4th ed. (1709), Epistle Dedicatory, sig. A6. Cf. Edmund Calamy, *A Caveat against New Prophets* (1708), p. 54; Josiah Woodward, *Remarks on the Modern Prophets* (1708). Hickes was a nonjuror: he had refused to swear allegiance to William and Mary after the Glorious Revolution. Hickes, a High Churchman, Calamy, a Presbyterian, and Woodward, a Latitudinarian, all had the same fears for the safety of true religion.

34. Defoe, *Review of the State of the English Nation*, vol. 5, no. 12 (April 24, 1708), p. 48, and vol. 5, no. 32 (June 10, 1708), p. 125.

35. *A Letter from Dr. Emes to the MOB, Assembled at his Grave* (1708), p. 4.

36. Woodward, *The Copy of a Letter to Mr. F[rancis] M[oult]* (1708), pp. 9–10.

what strange and obstinate Conceits have seized Men, touching their Inspiration, what strange Motions, melancholy and distempered Imaginations have produced, and what Fallacies imposed upon the Judgment."[37] Benjamin Hoadly, Anglican Low Churchman and controversialist, youngest critic of the French Prophets (1676–1761), proposed medical explanation as a clear alternative to possession: "Persons may have what you call *Prophetical involuntary Motions*, and *Agitations*, by the Force of Nature, under the Power of a distempered Mind; without the Assistance of any superior Spirit, whether good or bad."[38] Instead of being overcome by unnatural forces, the French Prophets were victims of natural forces and human weakness. By the turn of the seventeenth century, physician as well as philosopher had mastered the alphabet of frailty.

Contemporary diagnosis of mind-related disorders (hysteria, melancholy, vapors, hypochondria, insanity) allowed for symptoms so various that critics could with ease place the physical/mental disturbances of the French Prophets in a vague but coherent medical context. Madness, for example, was presaged by "violent Fears, a Tremor and shaking of the Nerves, a new Turn of the Eye, confused Thoughts, Starts, and sudden Fits of speaking, and a declination of the Voice, amazing Dreams, deep Sighs, and a continued dread of Damnation."[39] The vapors affected people with an equally extensive set of symptoms, many of them obviously parallel to the agitations of the French Prophets. Beset by vapors or hysteric fits, people "have a difficulty in Breathing, and think they feel something that comes up into their Throat, which is ready to choke them; they struggle; cry out; make odd and inarticulate Sounds, or Mutterings; they perceive a Swimming in their Heads; a Dimness comes over their Eyes; they turn pale; are scarce able to stand; their Pulse is weak; they shut their Eyes; fall down, and remain senseless for some time."[40] Hypochondria, frenzy, and the forms of epilepsy each made themselves known by signs which might afford com-

37. Bayly, *An Essay upon Inspiration*, pp. 77, 408–9.
38. Hoadly, *A Brief Vindication of the Antient Prophets* (1709), p. 18.
39. Fallowes, *Method for the Cure of Lunatics*, p. 7 (all in italics in the original). Cf. especially Robert S. Kinsman, "Folly, Melancholy, and Madness: A Study in Shifting Styles of Medical Analysis and Treatment, 1450–1675," in *The Darker Vision of the Renaissance*, ed. Kinsman, UCLA Center for Medieval and Renaissance Studies, Contributions, 6 (Berkeley, 1974), pp. 273–320.
40. John Purcell, *A Treatise of Vapours*, 2d ed. (London, 1707), p. 708.

parisons with the convulsions of Jean Cavalier or the intimate sensations of John Lacy.[41] Some "Expert and Famous Doctors, that have an Exquisite Knowledge of the Structure of the Human Bodies, and what Movements Nature alone can produce in every Part," observed nothing supernatural in the motions of the French Prophets. The Huguenot pastor Jean Blanc, before referring to the doctors, asked rhetorically, "What is there Divine I pray you in the Shakings and Tossings of their Bodies, in their Tremblings, in their Agitations, in their Transports, in their Falls, in their Howlings, and generally in the diverse Symptoms that accompany their pretended Ecstasies? Can't all this proceed from Natural Causes? May it not be performed by art? And may it not be affected?"[42] Apart from his comments on art and affectation, Blanc's attitude was that of the majority of younger English critics and all Huguenot critics. If they differed on the precise natural cause, this was because many disorders were not better understood than were the animal spirits which "explained" them.

Francis Lee, physician and Philadelphian, fellow of the Royal Society and author of an excellent but critical history of the Montanists, concerned himself with the "Fevers of the Mind." Lee, who set up the second-century Christian schismatics as a parallel to the French Prophets, found that the Montanists and other enthusiasts had been victims of such fevers, which might "put forth themselves in as great a variety of Symptoms as the Hysterical and Hypochondriacal, if not in greater." Lee then propounded the essential medical analysis upon which many critics based their explanations: "But there is no Enthusiasm of any sort without a Fever in the Soul, though it may be complicated indeed with other Distempers besides. This seems to be seated chiefly in the Animal Spirits, as that of the Body in the Mass of the Blood."[43]

Whether one took the French Prophets to be frenzied, melancholic, distracted, hysterical, intoxicated by fancies, or just plain mad, one assumed an underlying "Fever in the Soul."[44] The

41. See, for example, David Irish, *Levamen Infirmi* (London, 1700), p. 44; Benjamin Allen, *The Natural History of the Chalybeat* (London, 1699), p. 73 et passim; Owsei Temkin, *The Falling Sickness*, 2d ed. (Baltimore, 1971), pp. 169, 224.

42. Blanc, *A Preservative against False Prophets* (1708), p. 8. I have been unable to locate the names of the physicians referred to or their report(s).

43. A Lay Gentleman [Francis Lee], *The History of Montanism* (1709), p. 345; *Dictionary of National Biography* 11:792–93.

44. Cf. *Observations upon Elias Marion* (1707), pp. 7–8 [hysteric], p. 14 [melan-

medical theory of the behavior of the French Prophets internalized the prime irritant: physicians and critics replaced the fiery demons of hell with the "Sulphurous saline Animal Spirits," overheated and overpowering. There was a distinct echo of evil spirits in the writer William King's sketch of the work of animal spirits during false inspiration:

> Unusual Warmth first kindled in the Brain,
> Diffus'd, like Lightning shoots thro' every Vein.
> Whilst in their Breast the Immaterial Fire,
> Fed on its self, boils up the Fevre higher,
> And Lambent Flames from every Pore transpire.

For those disposed to medical explanations, possession was still a viable diagnosis or analogy; animal spirits, acting on "natural" principles which scarcely differed from the supernatural, were substituted for the devil and his legions. Human behavior was consequently explicable even at its most bizarre by the action of forces ultimately under human control.[46]

Medical theory covered not only the agitations of the French Prophets but also their supposed miracles and supra-normal powers. The parallel with demonic possession was exact, as if medical terms were but euphemisms for the wiles of the devil. Like the possessed, the diseased were capable of extraordinary and impossible deeds. The insane had long been treated as impervious to cold and capable of acts otherwise incredible; Francis Hutchinson suggested that the prophet John Lacy had glided across a room by the inordinate strength of a madman.[47] The traits of the possessed and the insane

---

cholic]; Nicholson, *Falsehood of New Prophets*, p. 29 [distracted]; Lee, *History of Montanism*, p. 80 [frenzy]; Kingston, *Enthusiastic Impostors*, 1:121 [intoxicated].

45. William Salmon, *Iatricia: Seu Praxis Medendi* (London, 1694), p. 771, on the "Sulphurous saline Animal Spirits"; [William King], *The Prophets: an Heroic Poem* (1708), canto 3. The author of this last tract was identified by Frank Christol in his "Une affaire sensationelle: le prophétisme camisard en Angleterre," uncatalogued typescript and manuscript in brown paper package, Papiers Christol, Bibliothèque de la Société pour l'Histoire du Protestantisme français (Paris).

46. Medical explanations were current among the less literate also. In York, an apothecary refused to believe that the agitations of one French Prophet were other than a convulsive fit, and he bled the poor prophet by force (*Historical Manuscripts Commission Reports*, vol. 63: Egmont D.1, 32). Baptists in London, finding a French Prophet under ecstasy in their meetinghouse, scurried to dose him with seltzer water: B.P.U.G., MSS fr. 605, letter of Oct. 27, 1719.

47. Hutchinson, *Short View*, p. 19. Cf. Bayly, *An Essay upon Inspiration*, p. 413. John Lacy was one of the few French Prophets to be directly accused of insanity. His

were applied by critics to victims (like the prophets) of other mind-related disorders. Philadelphus answered the arguments of one French Prophet, a prosperous chemist named Francis Moult, "Had you read more of Physic, and less of Jacob Behmen [Boehme], you might find several instances of *Men*, *Women*, and *Children* acted by *Involuntary Motions* in Hysteric Fits, nay, Sing to perfection, though in their natural State of Health, never could Sing, the least Note, Climb up Walls like Cats, and do abundance of such Prodigious wonderful Actions."[48] Thus opponents explained the prophets' unusual fluency of speech and elegance of language as the products of Fancy impregnated by violent animal spirits. Miraculous cures were understood to be the result of desire and mental impressions, for "Strange are the Influences of the Passions upon the Body." A physician proposed a medical diagnosis for the famous tears of blood wept in the Cévennes, and Camisard *inspirés* were said to have prophesied from the effusions of a vaporous and whimsied brain disarrayed by excessive fasting, worry, and fear.[49]

The vagaries of mental disorder and soul-body imbalance could not, however, furnish an adequate explanation for the ability of the French Prophets to effect cures on others or to work miracles in which others believed. These social elements could not be sufficiently accounted for by personal malady. The majority of critics once more resorted to natural (if practically ethereal) causes to make sense of socially extravagant behavior.

The faculty in each human being which permitted of intense social sympathy was the imagination. The part of the soul most accessible to the animal spirits, it could be stirred up by a disorder in the brain as fiery particles coursed through cranial passages. Like animal spirits, the imagination too might be described as irregular; like the

wife supposedly took legal action to have him declared insane, but there is no record thereof in the appropriate Chancery papers. See Archives Etrangères (Paris), Corr. Politique, Angleterre, vol. 223, fols. 51–51v.; Kingston, *Enthusiastic Impostors*, 1:39, 51; Edmund Chishull, *Great Danger and Mistake of all New Uninspired Prophecies* (1708), p. 44. Nicholson, *Falsehood of New Prophets*, pp. 28–29, states that the believer Robert Wise was put into Bedlam for his adherence to the French Prophets, but again there is no record of his admission in the Admissions Book, 1702–15, of the Archives of the Bethlem Royal Hospital (Beckenham).

48. G. Philadelphus, *An Answer to the Right Way of Trying Prophets* (1708), p. 13.

49. Josiah Woodward, *An Answer to the Letter of John Lacy* (1708), p. 28; *Reflections on Sir Richard Bulkeley's Answer to Several Treatises* (1708), pp. 56–57; *A Dissuasive against Enthusiasm* (1708), pp. 45–46; Bayly, *An Essay upon Inspiration*, p. 389; Jean Graverol, *Réflexions désintéressées sur certains prétendus inspirez*, 2 parts (1707), 2:38.

mind, the imagination might be depraved. It was the faculty through which many social emotions (admiration, wonder, envy, affection) were registered in the human frame.[50]

"Nothing is more difficult in medicine," wrote the sixty-year-old Huguenot pastor Claude Groteste de la Mothe, "than to explain the strength or the weakness of the imagination." Somehow it had power enough to register upon an unborn child the fright of its pregnant mother; it was often so weak that casual suggestion might prompt involuntary mimicry.[51] The special sensitivity of the imagination governed the influence of one human being upon another. Feeble persons (mentally or physically) were liable to a kind of contagion, a "Distemper of the Imagination," a tendency to imitate whatever made a strong positive impression upon their fancy.[52] The French Prophets, according to most of their critics, appealed to people on the principle of imitation, playing upon the susceptibility of a disabled or overwrought imagination: "As one gapes seeing another gaping, and as one Grape does *livorem ducere* from its Fellow; so does a Man, strongly impressed by his Sight of these Men in such Fits fall into the same, even when he knows not how, by a kind of Irresistible Imitation."[53] Henry Nicholson, as an erstwhile French Prophet who had himself experienced agitations, accepted this theory of contagious imitation to make his own case comprehensible: "Yet for the space of six weeks I could neither see any of the Motions of the Prophets, or even think of them, without some irregular Motions, caused by some such involuntary Instigations, as the Nerves are affected withal when we behold a Person yawning, to imitate the Motion we see in another."[54]

As the person was possessed by evil spirits or animal spirits, so the body politic might be possessed by the spirit of imitation, uncontrolled imagination. This was the essential thrust of the word

50. Cf. *British Apollo*, vol. 1, no. 31 (May 26–28, 1708); Nicholson, *Falsehood of New Prophets*, p. 13; Marc Vernous, *A Preservative Against the False Prophets*, p. 48.
51. Groteste de la Mothe, *Caractère des nouvelles prophecies* (1708), p. 89; Keith, *Magick of Quakerism*, p. 73. The Chronological Diary of the *Historical Register* (July 1714–Jan. 1716), p. 59, for May 17, 1715, noted the case of a woman who gave birth to a child "on the forehead of which was the plain Mark of the Eclipse that happened the 22nd of April preceding." The eclipse had frightened the mother.
52. Cf. N. N., *An Account of the Lives and Behaviour of the Three French Prophets*, pp. 33–34.
53. Humfrey, *Account*, p. 6; Bayly, *An Essay upon Inspiration*, pp. 409–10.
54. Nicholson, *Falsehood of New Prophets*, p. 14.

"enthusiasm," for by the early eighteenth century enthusiasm as a reference to religious behavior was primarily a term for disease of the body politic rather than of the individual.[55] Where before the Huguenot physician Meric Casaubon had associated enthusiasm with personal mental disorders, now critics investigated the social factors.

In the most popular dictionary of his age, the *Glossographia* (1656), Blount defined enthusiasm as "an inspiration, a ravishment of the spirit, divine motion, Poetical fury."[56] Blount's definition was the first to introduce the religious aspect, the pretension to divine inspiration which was the customary meaning of the earlier word, "fanaticism." In response perhaps to the social disturbances occasioned by Civil War "fanatics," Commonwealth and Restoration writers tagged "enthusiasm" with the religious and social implications of "fanaticism." Edward Phillips, in his *New World of Words* (1658), defined "enthusiasts" not as individuals but as "a certain Sect of people which pretended to the Spirit and Revelations."[57] Meric Casaubon, insisting upon physiological causes, considered the enthusiast as an individual medical case. With some help from Robert Burton's *Anatomy of Melancholy* (1621), Casaubon determined that enthusiasm was "an extraordinary, transcendent, but natural fervency, or pregnancy of the soul, spirits, or brain, producing strange effects, apt to be mistaken for supernatural." Enthusiasm was incidental to other transcendent but natural diseases: melancholy, madness, frenzy, epilepsy, hysteria.[58] The Cam-

---

55. Edmund Calamy explained the progress of a delusion from personal to social: "Hereupon they admired them as the Peculiar Favourites of Heaven; and Admiration we all know has a transforming Power. Admiring them, they wished they might be like them; wished they might be favoured of Heaven as much as they: And what more natural? From wishing they came to praying to God that it might be so: And by Degrees the Fancy being elevated, and the Natural Spirits strangely Agitated, they first tried to imitate them, and then fancied they were like them, and as much inspired as they" (*Caveat*, p. 30). Cf. Groteste de la Mothe, *Caractère*, p. 91.

56. Cited by George Williamson, "The Restoration Revolt against Enthusiasm," in his *Seventeenth-Century Contexts* (Chicago, 1961), p. 216.

57. Abraham P. Persky, "The Changing Concept of Enthusiasm in the 17th and 18th Centuries" (Ph.D. diss., Stanford University, 1959), pp. 19–24; Susie Irene Tucker, *Enthusiasm: A Study in Semantic Change* (Cambridge, 1972), pp. 15–16; *Oxford English Dictionary* 4:59, "Fanatic."

58. Meric Casaubon, *A Treatise concerning Enthusiasm* (London, 1655), pp. 17, 28–29. Cf. Clarence M. Webster, "Swift and Some Earlier Satirists of Puritan Enthusiasm," *Publications of the Modern Language Association* 48 (1933):

bridge Platonist Henry More, in defense of the true enthusiasm by which contemplative religion was ennobled, had also supposed false enthusiasts to be ill: "The *Spirit* then that wings the *Enthusiast* in such a wonderful manner," he wrote in his *Enthusiasmus Triumphatus* (1656), "is nothing else but the Flatulency which is in the *Melancholy* complexion, and rises out of the *Hypochondriacal* humour upon some occasional heat." One cured enthusiasm by temperance, humility, and reason.[59] John Locke, at the end of the century, discerned no explanation for enthusiasts other than some melancholy or affected fancy, for who but the mentally disordered would be unwilling to exercise proper reason and so avoid enthusiasm? If the enthusiast was not ignorant, he was not well, doing "violence to his own faculties."[60] Whatever one's theological bent—Platonism, deism, orthodoxy—or religious connection, the medical analysis of enthusiasm seemed to solve many problems of human behavior.

The medical perception of enthusiasm continued throughout the period in tandem with a fear of the religious enthusiast and a belief that insanity—to which enthusiasm was related—was an illness treatable by human means. The increasing designation of hospitals for the insane in the eighteenth century would be an expression of social fears and medical rationalism: to keep the mad away from society but within distance of human treatment. Many critics of the French Prophets had a parallel view of religious enthusiasts, and John Tutchin, editor of *The Observator*, made the parallel explicit. He proposed the construction of a religious bedlam (Royal Bethlem lunatic hospital) for the French Prophets and their counterparts. Religious enthusiasts endangered society and the church, but they could not be handled by the rigidity of the law: "For what law can

---

1142. F.-Maximilien Misson, *Sentimens désintéressez* (1710), p. 54n, commented on Casaubon's *Treatise*: "mais pour dire franchement la vérité, ce Livre est une Rapsodie fort indigeste, et fort abondants en contradictions."

59. More, *Enthusiasmus Triumphatus*, in *A Collection of Several Philosophical Writings of Henry More* (London, 1662), p. 12 (Section XVII), p. 18 (Section XXI). More said that he omitted mention of satanic agency because the devil's "Causality is more vagrant, more lax and general than to be brought in here" (p. 48). On the Cambridge Platonists, see especially Rosalie L. Colie, *Light and Enlightenment* (Cambridge, 1957).

60. Locke, *An Essay Concerning Human Understanding*, ed. A. C. Fraser, 2 vols. (New York, 1959), 2:430, bk. 4, chap. 19, "Of Enthusiasm," which first appeared in the 4th ed. (1700).

control or rectify Nature? And is it not unjust to prosecute one Person, because he has not so much Reason as another?"[61]

That which put enthusiasm into the category of a social disease was the medical analogy of contagion. The infective power of religious enthusiasm became an integral part of the definition of enthusiasm in general. Contagion was the medical equivalent of a demonic possession of the body politic, and animal spirits, morally neutral, once again were substituted for evil spirits.

The Royal Society had in the 1680s discussed the scientific aspects of a "contagious Communication of a strong Imagination."[62] In 1707, the Quaker-turned-Anglican George Keith (1639–1716) attempted to put the discussion of religious enthusiasm on a scientific plane. Revealing the dispositions of a man not yet done with the idea of possession, he distinguished natural from divine and demonic enthusiasms. Natural enthusiasm, he wrote, was the product of "some natural Magic, Fascination or Magnetism" conveyed from person to person by "certain Animal Subtile Effluviums."[63] The eighty-seven-year-old John Humfrey, more committed than Keith to the possibility of possession, argued like him that since there was undeniably an "Efflux of Spirits, Particles, or Atoms, from one Body to another" in fevers, "why may we not conceive an *Effluvium* of some Immaterial Spirits from the Mind of one Man, as of Material from the Body! And as the one prevails to the affecting another's Body with these Fits and Agitations, so may the other to the affecting the Soul with the same Passions, Belief, and Imagination."[64] The Quaker George Whitehead, writing against his former friend Keith, perceived that the notion of effluvium was a sort of magic best left to students of conjury. John Lacy too mocked the "Corpuscular Philosophy," which made animal volatile spirits into corporeal beings, as a "sort of Natural Magic."[65] Nevertheless, younger critics seemed to accept the hypothesis of effluvia, though

61. *The Observator*, July 23–26, 1707; cf. August 6–9, 1707. See also John Brydall, *Non compos mentis; or the Law relating to Natural fools, Mad folks and Lunatick Persons* (London, 1700). Cf. Michel Foucault, *Folie et déraison* (Paris, 1961), translated from an abbreviated French edition as *Madness and Civilization*, trans. Richard Howard (New York, 1965).

62. Royal Society (London), MSS Early Letters, H. 3.72, Letter to Robert Plot from Richard Huntington, read January 16, 1684.

63. Keith, *Magick of Quakerism*, table of contents, Sec. 5, and p. 37.

64. Humfrey, *Account*, p. 8.

65. George Whitehead, *Power of Christ Vindicated* (1708), p. 163; Lacy, *General Delusion*, p. 411.

they probably preferred the more "scientific" phrasing of deist
John Trenchard. He prefaced his discussion with a reference to
Newtonian theory: "Every thing in Nature is in constant Motion,
and perpetually emitting Effluviums and minute Particles of its Substance, which operate upon, and strike other Bodies. . . . And the
poisonous and melancholy Vapours streaming from an enthusiast,
cause Distraction and Raving as well as the Bite of a Mad Dog."[66]
Deist or orthodox, opponents of the French Prophets believed that
the animal spirits within the body were somehow, like the soul in
Jonathan Swift's analysis of religious enthusiasm, launched out.[67]

Whatever his eloquence, Anthony Ashley Cooper, third earl of
Shaftesbury (1671–1713), had not strayed as far from traditional
views as he might have wished in his *Letter concerning Enthusiasm*.
He accepted ready-made the image of contagion which physicians
and clergymen together had fashioned. The "Panic" of enthusiasm
among the French Prophets operated in social situations, as Shaftesbury described it, much as animal spirits or evil spirits worked in the
body, and with equal mystery. Mary Astell (under the pseudonym of
William Wotton) made fun of Shaftesbury's claim that "Looks are
infectious," and Edward Fowler now prepared to plug his ears and
nose and shield his eyes when observing enthusiasts.[68] Another
respondent to the *Letter* had a more acute comment: Shaftesbury
was slick but logically inconsistent. According to this anonymous
author, Shaftesbury's exposition of enthusiasm was circular,
incapable of explaining how the infection originated in the individual
or why it affected one rather than another.[69] This comment under-
scores Shaftesbury's particular contribution to the development of
the idea of enthusiasm. The *Letter* demonstrated no clear understanding of individuals but skillfully wedded all enthusiasm to social

66. John Trenchard (with Thomas Gordon?), *The Natural History of Superstition*
(London, 1709), pp. 13, 19–20.

67. Jonathan Swift, *A Discourse concerning the Mechanical Operation of the Spirit
in a Letter to a Friend* (1704), p. 291. Despite a caricature of animal spirits as a
"Crowd of little Animals, but with Teeth and Claws extremely sharp," Swift finally
explained enthusiasm as a "mere spontaneous Impulse" to imitate others in a highly
emotional environment (pp. 299, 304). Cf. Tucker, *Enthusiasm*, p. 68. The Greek
beliefs in effluvia had been resurrected in the seventeenth century by scientists
puzzling out magnetic and electric phenomena. See Hesse, *Forces and Fields*, pp.
88–90, 100, 117.

68. William Wotton [Mary Astell], *Bart'lemy Fair* (1709), pp. 164–65; [Fowler],
Reflections Upon a Letter concerning Enthusiasm, pp. 61–62.

69. *Remarks on the Letter to a Lord concerning Enthusiasm*, pp. 53–55.

contagion. Like other good writers, Shaftesbury was able to advance a common thesis with striking emphasis, but the mystery (and the weakness of analysis) remained. Borrowing the metaphor of fire and tinder, Shaftesbury wrote that "Panic" spread as the imagination was inflamed: "The combustible Matters lie prepared within, and ready to take fire at a spark; but chiefly in a Multitude served with that Spirit. No wonder if the blaze arises so of a sudden; when innumerable Eyes glow with the Passion, and heaving Breasts are laboring with Inspiration: When not the Aspect only, but the very Breath and Exhalations of Men are infectious, and the inspiring Disease imparts it self by insensible Transpiration."[70] As a satisfactory explanation of religious enthusiasm, "insensible Transpiration" left much to be desired and resembled Swift's noted "perspiration of the Spirit," to avoid which some enthusiasts wore quilted caps.[71] Shaftesbury had dressed in fine language the belief of the reviewer Sophronius that "Enthusiasm *Sows it self*, and like the blood of a Wart cut off, brings twenty for one."[72]

The *Letter* achieved notoriety because its deist author took seriously the notion of enthusiasm as a social disease and proposed a social physic: ridicule. Having recently heard John Lacy deliver a warning in poor Latin, Shaftesbury suggested that social mockery would be more effective against the French Prophets than legal prosecution. He relegated them to the broad satire of the puppet booths in Bartholomew Fair.[73] Ricicule would expose the enthusiasts to the only true antidote, *"our cold dead Reasonings,"* compounded like some bitter remedy with the syrup of good-natured sarcasm.[74]

Thus far, the hypotheses about the behavior of the French Prophets had in common the postulate that they were sincere people

70. Anthony Ashley Cooper, third earl of Shaftesbury, *A Letter concerning Enthusiasm* (1708), pp. 68–69. I am stressing the common ground of conceptions about human behavior between deist and orthodox Christian. Contrast Manuel, *Eighteenth Century Confronts the Gods*, pp. 62, 71, 81; George Rosen, "Enthusiasm 'a dark Lanthorn of the spirit,'" *Bulletin of the History of Medicine* 42 (1966):420–21; Persky, "Changing Concepts of Enthusiasm," pp. 54–70.

71. Swift, *Mechanical Operation of the Spirit*, p. 304.

72. *Censura Temporum*, vol. 1 (June 1708), p. 168.

73. Shaftesbury, *Letter concerning Enthusiasm*, pp. 43, 71; Fatio Calendar, July 5, 1707. On Bartholomew Fair—whose advertisements for 1707–19 are missing—see Sybil Rosenfeld, *The Theatre of the London Fairs in the 18th Century* (Cambridge, 1960), pp. 4–21.

74. Cf. Shaftesbury's *Several Letters written by a Noble Lord to a Young Man at the University* (London, 1716), pp. 4–6.

overcome by a rather indefinable but material force. The shift from demonic possession to disease and social enthusiasm as the prevailing explanations reflected an increased capacity on the part of critics to assign culpability. The possessed and the insane could not be held responsible for their acts, and Casaubon did not hold the zealot guilty for bizarre acts when plainly a medical case.[75] Henry More, partisan of rationality, had declared the enthusiasts partly guilty; though sincere and often predisposed to melancholy, enthusiasts could (if they *would*) refrain from strange behavior. Religious enthusiasts were persons in whom reason had lost control, and critics of the French Prophets early suspected them of a willingness to relinquish the guidance of reason. Either by admiration and desire, by some sponge-like disposing of the soul, or by indulgence of the imagination, people submitted voluntarily to the mysterious effluvia.[76] Daniel Defoe, addressing the French Prophets after the failure of Emes's resurrection, which he thought should have dispelled all delusion, wrote: "The Charm is now over, the Snare is broken, and if ye please you are escaped; *if you will not escape, no Body can help that*; not to abandon these pretences now, would be to profess your selves willingly imposed upon, and that you court the Delusion, even as such."[77] Critics compiled long lists of other religious enthusiasms throughout history, from Montanus to John Mason, to show that the French Prophets' actions were well within a certain spectrum of recurrent human behavior. The lists of enthusiasm were meant in part to imply that some sincere people in each age had courted delusion. If one did not attribute all earlier instances to possession or madness, then there was ample scope to lay at least some of the responsibility for their behavior upon the enthusiasts themselves.[78]

Restrained by a belief in the sincerity of the French Prophets and by a psychology of animal spirits, most critics could not hold the prophets or their followers fully responsible for what they did. "Irrational" behavior, though explicable without recourse to the

75. Casaubon, *A Treatise concerning Enthusiasme*, pp. 88–89; Webster, "Swift and Some Earlier Satirists of Puritan Enthusiasm," p. 1144.

76. More, *Enthusiasmus Triumphatus*, pp. 46–47; Calamy, *Caveat*, p. 30; *Reflections on Sir Richard Bulkeley's Answer*, pp. 36–37; Bayly, *An Essay upon Inspiration*, p. 411.

77. Defoe, *Review*, vol. 5, no. 33 (June 12, 1708), p. 131.

78. The longest list of enthusiasms is in *The Devil of Delphos* (1708), which arrives at the "Present Pretended Prophets" after 74 pages of other "enthusiasts."

divine or the demonic, was still associated with the uncontrollable effluvia that spread from the corners of life.[79]

CUNNING DEVICES

Those opponents of the French Prophets who challenged their sincerity were those who perceived in them a prevailing rationality. They explained the behavior of the French Prophets as part of a subtle plot, a well-designed imposture in which curious agitations were misleading showpieces. The deception hypothesis admitted effluvia on occasion to account for the success of the imposture, but the point of the hypothesis was to translate seemingly irrational behavior into rational terms by detecting a set of rational, if evil, purposes.

The clues, according to the anonymous and influential author of the *Clavis Prophetica* (1707), were in the carriage of that rational mathematician Nicolas Fatio. Fatio, it appeared, had not lost his senses but was deploying new tactics to promote religious skepticism. Distrusting the mathematician's religious conversion in the early 1690s as too abrupt, the anonymous author feared that behind the artifice of the puppet prophets stood a devious and intelligent puppet-master: "A Man who has bid defiance to all Religion, grows on a sudden wondrous fond of the Cabalistical Art; discovers these things in the Scriptures which no Body else can see there, and finds Mountains of Sciences in every Syllable of that Book which he before despised. The overacting of his Part is very much to be suspected; the Mind of Man does not go so fast from one Extreme to another; it looks all like Design and Artifice. They who have had a mind to deceive themselves, will say, The Man is an Enthusiast; we must pardon him these little Ravings. But others draw from hence very different Inferences, and think they see clearly in this new jargon, a studied Affectation, much more dangerous than an open and avowed Defense of Spinoza."[80] So people were overcome by

---

79. Cf. Manuel, *Eighteenth Century Confronts the Gods*, p. 71. A few did dispute the existence of animal spirits: George Cheyne, *The English Malady* (London, 1733), p. xxii; [John Harris], *A Letter to the Fatal Triumvirate* (London, 1719), p. 15. But see G. Bowles, "Physical, Human and Divine Attraction in the Life and Thought of George Cheyne," *Annals of Science* 31 (1974):473–88; Bastholm, *History of Muscle Physiology*, pp. 156, 170–73, 186–94.

80. *Clavis Prophetica; or, a Key to the Prophecies of Mons. Marion, and the other Camisars*, 2 parts (1707), 2:7, 21–22. On the meaning of the reference to Spinoza, see

the "cunning Devices of execrable Imposture," by the very power of reason.[81] Rational men, responsible and unpardonable, could sway others by playing upon the imagination, manipulating enthusiasm to nefarious ends. The power of this imposture lay in its boldness, the sheer impudence to counterfeit nothing less than divine prophecy.[82]

Advocates of the deception hypothesis regarded the French Prophets as too harmful to be other than impostors. The object of their plot, whether or not appreciated by the majority of believers, was to subvert revealed religion. According to a critic's age and personal suspicions, either Socinians, Spinozists (skeptics), deists, Jesuits, or atheists were the hidden jugglers.[83] Shaftesbury had been too kind to the French Prophets. It was but "sewing Pillows under Armholes," wrote Eubulus, to treat gently those who undermined the Christian religion.[84] To some critics, in fact, Shaftesbury's image of social enthusiasm itself jeopardized revealed religion by reducing all, including true faith, to "panic." His nonchalant diagnosis and remedy were just as fatal as the supposed disease. Seen in this way, Shaftesbury was as naïf as the too-trusting followers who never thought that the prophets might be insincere.[85]

Apart from the author of the *Clavis Prophetica* and the playwright

Rosalie Colie, "Spinoza in England, 1665–1730," *Proceedings of the American Philosophical Society* 107 (1963):183–219. Fatio's conversion from skepticism to Christianity is described in Charles Domson, "Nicolas Fatio de Duillier and the Prophets of London: An Essay in the Historical Interaction of Natural Philosophy and Millennial Belief in the Age of Newton" (Ph.D. diss., Yale University, 1972); Manuel, *A Portrait of Isaac Newton*, pp. 194, 199–202. Both have overlooked a letter from Fatio to his brother on the subject of Socinianism (December, 1707): "Je suis convaincu que la Doctrine des Unitaires approche moins de la vérité que ne fait la Doctrine connu sur la Trinité, quand elle est bien entendue" (B.P.U.G., MSS fr. 602, fol. 115).

81. *Reflection on Sir Richard Bulkeley's Answer*, p. 27; N.N., *Account of the Three French Prophets*, p. 2.

82. Cf. Groteste de la Mothe, *Caractère*, p. 22.

83. Ibid., p. 45 (Socinians); Humfrey, *Farther Account*, p. 16 (Jesuits); Calamy, *Caveat*, p. 40, and *Censura Temporum*, vol. 1 (April 1708), pp. 108–9 (Catholics); Hutchinson, *Short View*, p. 39 (atheists); Merlin [Clement Rémy?], *Ancienne prédiction* (London, 1708?), p. 8 (deists). The older the critic, the readier to suspect Catholic plots; the younger critics feared freethinkers. Huguenots feared both equally.

84. *Censura Temporum*, vol. 2 (October 1709), p. 692.

85. [Fowler], *Reflections Upon a Letter concerning Enthusiasm*, p. 9; cf. Hoadly, *Brief Vindication*, preface. Persky notes that Shaftesbury's deism had implicit in it a belief in an inner light (to perceive moral laws) not much different from the enthusiast's inner light: "The Changing Concepts of Enthusiasm," p. 82. Cf. *An Appeal from the Prophets to their Prophecies*, p. 12.

A SONG in the fourth Act of the Modern Prophets.

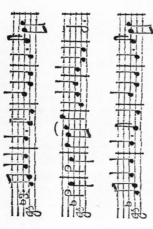

ELevate your joys, ye infpir'd of the Town,
  The *Camizars* are come, are come ;
To Inftruct and confute the black Gown,
  Germany and *France* have been dancing the Jigg:
And now they fain, they fain, they fain,
  Would new model the *Tory* and *Whigg*;
They Preach and they Pray, the Spirit moves,
And then they fhake, and quake, and *Gambols* they play,
    This Divine they call,
And gathers up the Mob, the Devil and all.

Pillorys we laugh at, and Infamy there,
  The lofs of Ears, and Lafh
We Frantickly think is an Honour to bear ;
  Round about the Nation thus Madly we go,
And where we find the Fools
  Are moft Fertile, our Tenets we fow:
    A change we'd obtain,
Which to effect we hum and ha, and Profelytes gain:
    Eagerly they come,
And Joyn to promote Rebellion at home.

One of the songs from Thomas d'Urfey's play, *The Modern Prophets*, from his *Songs Compleat, Pleasant and Divertive; set to Musick by Dr. John Blow, Mr. Henry Purcell, and other Excellent Masters of the Town* (London, 1719).

Tom d'Urfey, the foremost advocates of the deception hypothesis were émigré Huguenots.[86] The French Protestant ministers who wrote against the French Prophets were men unfamiliar with post-Revocation France. They had not witnessed miracle or prophecy in Languedoc, but saw only the riots in their London communities when Fage, Cavalier, and Marion came to England.[87] Whatever divine aid had been granted in France to persecuted Protestants bereft of a proper ministry, the actions of the *inspirés* in London were considered to be out of context and socially reprehensible. Huguenot opponents believed that the French Prophets encouraged anarchy, turning well-ordered churches into unseemly Babels, usurping the functions of ordained ministers as had been their custom in the "Desert." To the elder clergy, at least, the tradition of "Desert" prophecy was not applicable in England. Jean Cavalier's acrobatic convulsions and Marion's blistering judgments were inappropriate to their new environment. Whereas in the Cévennes belligerent prophecy and seizures had corresponded to a warring atmosphere and to physical sufferings of the faithful, in London only the occasional mobs might serve as justification for a similar posture. Many critics recognized the overreaction of the prophets in London; they carefully distinguished the "Desert" situation from that of Britain and allowed for the possibility of divine aid where God's children were actually persecuted, in France but not in England. Huguenot pastors, most directly menaced by the French Prophets, were unwilling to believe that the attempted transposition of the "Desert" into London parlors was only possession, disease, or enthusiasm. They doubted that the French Prophets, guided by the intelligence of Fatio and F.-Maximilien Misson, could not themselves realize the error of matching Cévenol prophecy to London Protestantism. They regarded the violence of the inspired as proof of a conspiracy against tender religion; the prophets were "Emissaries of a Foreign Power, Enemies to the State and Church."[88]

Since, for most, religion was the fundament of human society, a

86. Tom d'Urfey was of Huguenot descent. The author of the *Clavis Prophetica* probably had close associations with Huguenots, for he was one of only two critics whose attacks were translated from English into French. The other was Offspring Blackall (*La manière d'examiner les prophètes*, trans. J. R. [1708]).

87. The following ministers were all at least sixty years old in 1708: Marc Vernous, Jean Blanc, Jean Graverol, Claude Groteste de la Mothe, Jean-Armand Dubourdieu. D'Urfey was fifty-five.

88. *An Appeal from the Prophets to their Prophecies*, p. 22, N. N., *Account of the*

fear for the well-being of religion could easily become a fear for the survival of civil and social institutions. Led by rational, crafty gentlemen like Fatio, Misson, and Lacy, the lower classes would discard what little rationality they were supposed to command in favor of an impassioned onslaught against law, government, commerce, and social hierarchy. The drawn swords at the Hackney Marsh riot and the leveling principles of the prophet Abraham Whitrow and his disciple Sir Richard Bulkeley confirmed the social threat posed by the French Prophets.

Critics did indeed have some evidence that the French Prophets might tend toward political radicalism. Had not Marion and Lacy in 1706 and 1707 prophesied the burning of a great city? Had not Marion predicted that soon there would be "Overturnings of whole States, I tell thee. I will overturn them upside down"? Had not the English prophet Abraham Whitrow taken to heart the "Restitution of all things" and begun to advocate a widespread charity which closely resembled the doctrine of leveling, or spreading wealth equally? And had not Sir Richard Bulkeley in the summer of 1708 begun to implement the charity program with funds from his own estate? Yet these evidences were belied by the group's constant and consistent efforts to keep metaphors of destruction within the realm of personal spiritual transformation; Marion never once acted upon his prophecies as a guerilla leader initiating political warfare, and the French Prophets very quickly and publicly expelled Abraham Whitrow as a false prophet. Further, the group as a whole had no economic motive to restructure secular society, for despite comments to the contrary, the majority of believers were not poor, and the core of followers and prophets were well off.[89] Critics who

---

Three French Prophets, p. 29, and Humfrey, *Account*, pp. 15–16, all differentiate the situation in England from that in France. For Huguenot views summarized in this paragraph, see [Clement Rémy], *Sept dialogues entre deux frères* (May–July, 1707), 5:4; Graverol, *Réflexions désintéressées*, 1:22; Merlin, *Ancienne prédiction*, p. 5; Jean Blanc, *The Anathema of the False Prophets* (1708), pp. 8 (quotation), 12–13. Criticism of the miracles in the Cévennes was restrained, especially in English works, but see [Groteste de la Mothe], *Examen du théâtre sacré*; Spinckes, *New Pretenders to Prophecy Examined*, pp. 397–98.

89. Lacy, *Warnings*, 2:68, 70, 3:118; Marion, *Prophetical Warnings*, pp. 1, 7, 11–22, 60; *Clavis Prophetica*, vol. 1, throughout. On Whitrow, see Fatio Calendar, June–July 1708; Nicholson, *Falsehood of New Prophets*, pp. 18–19; Stack MSS lj: Historical Relation, fols. 39–40; Kingston, *Enthusiastick Impostors*, 2:111; Spinckes, *Pretenders Re-examined*, pp. xiii, 20–22, app. 3:51–56; George Berkeley, *Letters*, ed. A. A. Luce (London, 1956), p. 31; Abraham Whitrow, *Warnings of the Eternal Spirit* (London, 1709), pp. 166, 202, 278–79, 325, 329–30.

incorrectly emphasized the plebeian circumstances and revolutionary tendencies of most French Prophets were led to their exaggerations by the histories of the Levellers, the Ranters, and the Fifth Monarchists of the mid-seventeenth century. Some were simply making connections, by now traditional, among irrationality, enthusiasm, and the lower classes; others sought a connection between any and all millenarian beliefs and actions.[90] Although critics from all camps expressed concern over the social disruption likely to be caused by the new prophets, only those who stressed imposture viewed the disruption as deliberate. The imposture of enthusiasm posed a double threat, for there was then truly a method to the madness.

Sexual slander, overt in the frequent political allusion to the profligate Anabaptists of Münster in the 1530s, occurred most often in the works of critics who wished to demonstrate the insincerity of the prophets. Like unaccountable violence and the leveling principle, sexual misconduct was another example of social disturbance. At first, critics restricted sexual innuendo to character assassination, to prove the prophets immoral and untrustworthy. Cavalier, they implied, was completely degenerate, a despicable homosexual during his early months in London and then the eager husband of a woman of ill repute, the late prophet Jeanne Verduron. Fage, they said, was known for his debauchery among young women in the Cévennes; in London he too had hankered after Jeanne Verduron. Marion, wrote one author, used the powerful appeal of blessings to creep into widows' houses and "humouring those of that Sex, *that are laden with diverse Lusts*; preys upon their Bodies."[91]

90. *Clavis Prophetica*, 1:iii–iv; Keith, *Magick of Quakerism*, p. 82; Spinckes, *Pretenders Re-examined*, pp. vi–xi; Calamy, *Caveat*, p. 13; *Observations upon Elias Marion*, pp. 9–10; d'Urfey, *The Modern Prophets* (London, 1709), preface, pp. 11, 26–27; Robert Calder, *A True Copy of Letters Past betwixt Mr. R. C. Minister of the Gospel and Mr. James Cuninghame of Barns* (Edinburgh, 1710), p. 72. For critics who saw the French Prophets as lower-class threats, see *Clavis Prophetica*, 1:i–ii; Hutchinson, *Short View*, pp. 39, 47–50; *Rehearsal of the Observator*, Dec. 3, 1707.

91. Kingston, *Enthusiastick Impostors*, 1:33, 69, 2:210–12; *Clavis Prophetica*, 2:34; [Rémy], *Sept dialogues*, 2:7–8; Merlin, *Ancienne prédiction*, pp. 1–2; N. N., *Account of the Three French Prophets*, pp. 26–28. In Kingston (2:101–2), even Fatio and Portales are slandered, Portales for getting a young gentlewoman with child and then deserting her, Fatio for enjoying the company of Henriette Allut, wife of Jean Allut, prophet and leader. Manuel, *Portrait of Newton*, chap. 9, does suggest that in fact the relationship between Isaac Newton and Nicolas Fatio could have been homosexual, but there is no evidence anywhere for heterosexual escapades on his part. Nor is there substance to the accusations against Portales, Marion, or Fage. Jean Cavalier

With the emergence of women followers and women prophets, especially Elizabeth Gray, critics leveled sexual accusations against the entire group. Contemporary medical theory once more provided a backdrop for suspicions. Physicians thought women more prone to hysteria than men to the comparable hypochondria. They considered women more impressionable (passionate) than men; their "natural Temper" would predispose females to a "too easy Credulity." Addison wrote of the mind as a "she" when describing enthusiastic imaginary rapture, but there was nothing so glorious as a "strong steady masculine piety."[92] Inevitably attracted by visionaries and enthusiasts, women (it was believed) added a certain emotional instability to religious groups. George Keith's "efflux and effluvium of Spirits" became a facile vehicle for carnal desires; one kind of zeal led to another, wrote Swift, for "Persons of a visionary Devotion, either Men or Women, are in their Complexion, of all others, the most amorous."[93] The combination of enthusiasm, the reputed instability of women, and the insincerity of the prophets would yield, almost naturally, sexual misconduct. Further, by permitting hysterical women to play such important roles in the group, the French Prophets were approving the worst tendencies in the supposed female character.

For advocates of the deception hypothesis, the shabby morality of the prophets (male and female) was more than a by-product of enthusiasm. It was an omen of the chaos which scheming men (always men) could unleash with specific intent. Quickly explained away by the sophistry of Fatio or Lacy, immorality seemed to be condoned within the group as another facet of the design to undermine true religion and hence the social fabric. What other explanation could there be for the fact that on November 16, 1707, an inspired woman had stripped in the back of the Sardinian (Roman Catholic) Chapel in Duke Street and run naked up to the altar af-

---

was the least predictable of the prophets and eventually became an apostate; there are more consistent accusations of sexual misconduct against him than any other, but still I have no firm evidence to settle the issue. From 1706 to 1710, the French Prophets did not live communally or advocate free love. They would later have some problems with adulterous relationships encouraged by inspirations.

92. *Spectator*, no. 201, October 20, 1711; Bernard de Mandeville, *A Treatise of the Hypochondriack and Hysterick Passions* (London, 1711), pp. 166, 172–73; Sydenham, *Compleat Method*, pp. 149–50; Vernous, *Preservative*, p. 46.

93. Swift, *Mechanical Operation of the Spirit*, pp. 320–21; Keith, *Magick of Quakerism*, pp. 47–48.

ter mass, "where she appeared in several Strange and Indecent Postures, and being seemingly full of the pretended Spirit, she did hold forth in a Powerful manner; and could by no means be prevailed upon to desist; but on the contrary, told them she was come to Reform the People, and bring them to a right understanding"?[94] If people could be blinded to the shocking conduct of the prophets and retain faith in their inspirations, what behavior might not the prophets sanction in the name of religion? If women assumed the right to instruct men in the ways of divine justice, what would happen to the sinews of the male clerical establishment? If clever men insinuated their highly emotional protégées into positions of respect, what would happen to society?[95]

Accusations of political and sexual impurity reflected the upsetting, ambiguous position of the French Prophets. The group was a pollution of the body politic because its prophets claimed a power to bless and to curse which usually resided in recognized political and religious authorities. The group was also seen as a pollution of the body social, for their unnatural sexual life was held to be paradigmatic of countersocial group life. The standards upon which a community decides to understand laws and Scripture as either literal or figurative were being constantly challenged by the actions of the inspired. Critics, unable to predict the manner in which the prophets would transform the traditional system of religious metaphors, expressed their discomfort in political and sexual terms.[96]

94. *The French Prophetess turned Adamite* (1707), reprinted with introduction by W. Sparrow Simpson in "Lincoln's Inn Fields: The French Prophetess," *Notes and Queries*, 6th ser. 11 (January 10, 1885):21–22. This woman may have been Elizabeth Gray, but the source which normally would identify the actors in prophetic actions (Fatio's Calendar) is, curiously, silent about the chapel episode.

95. *Clavis Prophetica*, 1:iv–vi; A Person of Honour, *A Confutation of the Prophets* (1708), p. 6. Cf. [King], *The Prophets*, canto 3; d'Urfey, *The Modern Prophets*; Kingston, *Enthusiastick Impostors*, 1:48, 73; Samuel Keimer, *Brand pluck'd from the Burning* (1718), pp. 54, 71, 109, 112–13; Vernous, *Preservative*, p. 28.

96. Cf. Mary Douglas, *Purity and Danger* (London, 1966); Natalie Zemon Davis, "The Rites of Violence: Religious Riot in Sixteenth-Century France," *Past and Present* 59 (1973):57–60. Cf. also a tract which was translated from the French and published in London in 1708, J. F. Osterwald, *The Nature of Uncleanness Considered*. Osterwald early cites Jeremy Taylor's *Rules and Exercises of Holy Living* (1650), sec. 2, chap. 2: "That there are some Spirits so Atheistical, and some so wholly possessed with a Spirit of Uncleanness, that they turn the most prudent and chast Discourses into Dirt, and filthy Apprehensions; like Cholerick Stomachs, changing their very Cordials and Medicines into Bitterness, and in a literal sense turning the Grace of God into Wantonness" (Osterwald, "To the Reader,"

PILLORY DISAPOINTED,

OR, THE

False PROPHETS Advancement.

To the Tune of Rotten Eggs, Turnop-Tops, Pieces of Dirt, & Brick-Batts.

Elias Marion, the head French Prophet, his Speech on the Scaffold, at the Royal Exchange in Cornhil, on Tuesday the 2d of December.

OH! Wicked Generation of Vipers, worse than the Unbelieving *Philistians*, that kill'd the great, strong & good Prophet *Sampson*; had I the Jaw-bone of an Ass in mine Hand, I would tell you heaps upon heaps, & instead of a Thousand I would lay Ten Thousands of you a sprawling like Toads in a Common-shore, or Crab-Lice on a Goats Back. Oh! you *British Infidels*, why woun't you believe the Moon's made of a Green Cheese? Why woun't you believe the *Foolishness of Preaching according to the Scripture?* Why will you not believe my *Prophesies* & *Lies*, which cost you nothing, rather than Buy a *Coblers Almanack Year after Year, Staff'd with nothing else?* Oh Foolish Generation, who has Bewitch'd you? Who has has hardned your Hearts against us, that comes to tell you more in an Hour then you'l find true in an Age? If you are Angry at our Advancement, come & take our Places & Welcome; Pray, Bretheren spare your Eggs, to make your Candles, & be not so free of your Turnop-Tops & Brick-Batts; I vow as I am a Prophet, & the Son of a Prophet, I don't require these Presents at your Hands: For as sure as a Maid of Thirty (if such a Miracle be found in your Dwellings) is desirous of something to keep her from the Dreadful Sentence of leading Apes in Hell; so sure shall I fall into a Damnable Fit & betray my Britcher, if the Prophets of the L----d or rather the D----l, be not suddenly taken down a Hole Lower, & discharged from this Honourable Foot-stool of Repentance. Oh!

the Heathenly Temple in *Barbican*, how art thou laid Waste & made a Wilderness, by the wild Beast of the Forrest, and Raga-muffens of the Desarts: How are thy once Glittering VVindows shattered in Pieces, & thy inward *Sanctuary* made a Habitation for *Owls* & *Crickets*, those *Ominous Creatures of Ill Luck*.

To conclude, let us still Endeavour to Cheat Fools, Oblige Knaves, Impose on the VVise, & Plague our Betters, to which the rest of the *False Prophets* Cryed, *AMEN*, Oh! Oh!

And thus when Prophets for the Devil Preach,
They get poor silly Fool within their Reach;
Make them believe Good Spirits does the Tricks
When Wise Men know it all comes from Old-Nick.
Mad Men bewitch'd, turn Prophets in their Fits,
And seem'd Inspir'd, the midd'out of their Wits.

"Pillory Disapointed, or the False Prophets Advancement. To the Tune of Rotten Eggs, Turnop-Tops, Pieces of Dirt, & Brick-Batts."

The long theological quarrels with the French Prophets were in an important sense equivalent to sexual slander. They rested on the same fears for the well-being of the Church and the body politic; they expressed the same determination to prove the prophets untrustworthy and often, by innuendo, impostors. Theologians treated the millenarian beliefs of the French Prophets as the product of overheated zeal for or inordinate application to the secrets of Scripture, resembling the madness to which scholars were prone after years of excessive study. Many critics described the prophecies and polemics of believers as incoherent theology, the harvest of a heated imagination, "a confused Heap of Thoughts, which have no Connexion, and which destroy one another: A frightful Gallimaufry of Ideas and Expressions without Order and Method: A monstrous Composition of Words put together pell mell."[97] Just as the French Prophets as a social group were anomalous, confusing, so too as philosophers they were not within the bounds of expected human discourse. Theological arguments perpetuated the image of the French Prophets as furious people overwhelmed by desire; the too-avid desire for knowledge, like concupiscence, might lead to erratic and socially distressing behavior.

The usual theological argument against the new prophets stressed their superfluity. The argument ran as follows. The Bible is perfectly sufficient unto salvation. After the age of the apostles, who prepared the New Testament, the discernible reason for divine inspiration ceased. Though it were the very last age, there would still be no pressing need for further prophecy. If, nevertheless, by God's goodness another set of messengers are sent, they must be come, like the last, the apostles, to add to Scripture. The French Prophets, however, preach nothing original and themselves make no claim to be founding new doctrine. Most of the time they preach the coming of the millennium, which scripture warns will be preceded by false prophets (e.g., Matt. 24:24) but nowhere states must be heralded by new true prophets. Of course, God might do as God wishes and inspire further messengers without humanly discernible reasons, but as the sober Presbyterian minister Edmund Calamy wrote, "I think we ought to make a wide Difference between what God may do if he

---

p. iii). Here the sexual, medical, and theological problems of the transformation of pure to impure are impressively confused.

97. Blanc, *Anathema*, p. 9. Cf. Humfrey, *Farther Account*, p. 37; *Devil of Delphos*, p. 85; Hutchinson, *Short View*, pp. 53–57; *Dissuasive*, p. 84.

pleases, and what his Word gives us just Reason to expect he will do."[98]

"Just Reason" governed the commentary of all varieties of critics, for they had no other means of trying the inspirations of prophets than by rational inquiry and comparison with scriptural guidelines. Even the simplest person, argued the Huguenot pastor Jean Blanc, adapting a favorite deist dictum, was capable of making the trial of the spirits, for "Scripture is a Light proportioned to the Capacities of all Men."[99] Conversely, the cryptic elements in the Bible surpassed the understanding of even the most intelligent; those who abandoned "just Reason" to pry into scriptural mysteries likely harbored the curiosity of a "wavering and doubtful Mind." Even the Son of God did not know the exact season for the millennium (Matt. 24:36), so it was with considerable temerity that these new prophets should be so precise in their early predictions, and that Christians would trust to them.[100]

Contemporary churchmen with a millenarian bent—Bishops William Lloyd and Edward Fowler, Anglican ministers Josiah Woodward and Edmund Chishull, William Whiston (ordained a deacon by Lloyd)—reacted to the French Prophets with animosity, in print and in private. Some of their opposition was due to justified alarm at being mistaken for supporters of the new millenarians. The French Prophets themselves had ranked Fowler and his wife among their followers, and John Lacy confessed that, before his first prophecies, the sole work he had read on the coming of the Kingdom was by Whiston.[101] In 1710, a cleric in Bishop Lloyd's diocese accused Lloyd of sympathizing with the new prophets.[102] Whiston

98. Calamy, *Caveat*, p. 11; cf. especially Spinckes, *Pretenders Re-examined*, p. 18. The most pithy examples of the argument sketched in this paragraph may be found in *Censura Temporum*, vol. 1 (April 1708), pp. 107–8, 114; Bayly, *An Essay upon Inspiration*, p. 12; *Devil of Delphos*, pp. 3, 6; Hoadly, *Brief Vindication*, p. 6; Blackall, *Way of Trying Prophets*, pp. 11, 16–19; Spinckes, *Pretenders Examined*, pp. 360–67; and cf. Bishop Lloyd to Sir Richard Bulkeley, "I am very certain that there is not in Scripture any one Prophecy of any inspiration from God that is ever to be expected after that which he hath given us in the Holy Scriptures," all underlined in letter of February 10, 1708: Worcester Record Office, BA 5230, microfilm of Lloyd Papers, app. II. 14, p. 2031.

99. Blanc, *Anathema*, p. 4.

100. *Devil of Delphos*, p. 6; Blanc, *Anathema*, pp. 5–6; Calamy, *Caveat*, p. 24; Hoadly, *Brief Vindication*, pp. 3–4.

101. Lacy, *Relation of Dealings*, p. 15, referring to Whiston, *An Essay on the Revelation of St. John* (London, 1706).

102. Borthwicke Institute (York), Sharp MSS, microfilm 3/0, cited in Jacob, *The Newtonians and the English Revolution 1689–1720*, p. 127.

had even been attacked on the same grounds as the French
Prophets, for, asked Sophronius, "does he not often speak with too
much Assurance and Security of a Millennial State? at least of its
near Approach?"[103]

Latitudinarians all, these churchmen had more than selfish
qualms about the French Prophets. There was more to their
opposition than jealousy over the proper chronology for the
millennium. Like many other critics, the Low Churchmen had
adopted the postulates of Newtonian mechanics, but they had
especially taken to heart the image of stability in the Newtonian universe. This they applied to church and society as well as to physics
and natural science. The coming of the millennium would preserve
rather than disturb the social and religious authorities. To Whiston,
to Lloyd, to Woodward, the Second Coming provided no excuse to
forego "just Reason" for a wild faith in new personal inspirations.
Judged from such a standpoint, the French Prophets seemed to
upset the harmony between nature and society, reason and faith.
The years of assiduous study which the churchmen had undertaken
to make sense of the language of the Book of Revelation also made
them skeptical of men and women who blithely claimed swift inside
knowledge of scriptural mysteries. The prophets and their followers
did not appear judicious in their analysis of the decisive balance in
Revelation between the figurative and the literal. Prophetic behavior
and prophetic language endangered the proper, sober preparation
for the end of the world.[104]

Whatever the state of the world, at the millennium the faithful
would know a comforting continuity, not the terrible chaos

103. *Censura Temporum*, vol. 1 (January 1707/8), pp. 19–20, review of Whiston's
Accomplishment of Scripture Prophecies (London, 1708). Cf. George Hickes to
Arthur Charlett, February 21, 1712: "I take Mr. Whiston to be a great Enthusiast, and
Enthusiasm always hinders the Enthusiast from being sensible to his vices, especially
those of the spiritual kind." Bodleian Library (Oxford), MSS Ballard 12, fol. 196.

104. Jacob, *Newtonians and the English Revolution*; idem, "The Church and the
Formulation of the Newtonian World-View," *Journal of European Studies* 1
(1971):128–48; idem, "Millenarianism and Science in the Late Seventeenth Century,"
Journal of the History of Ideas 37 (1976):335–42; M. C. Jacob and W. A. Lockwood,
"Political Millenarianism and Burnet's Sacred Theory," *Science Studies* 2
(1972):265–79; David Kubrin, "Newton and the Cyclical Cosmos: Providence and the
Mechanical Philosophy," *Journal of the History of Ideas* 28 (1967):325–46, reprinted
in *Science and Religious Belief: A Selection of Recent Historical Studies*, ed. C. A.
Russell (London, 1973), pp. 147–69; idem, "Providence and the Mechanical Philosophy: the Creation and Dissolution of the World in Newtonian Thought" (Ph.D.
diss., Cornell University, 1968), pp. 9, 77.

predicted and mimed by the prophets. Social bonds would not be loosened. There would be no paradise on earth, no material restoration before the final resurrection, wrote Woodward in answer to Sir Richard Bulkeley.[105] There would be no sudden dissolution of the world, Chishull assured his readers.[106] Even more perilous than preaching false but attractive doctrine about the millennium, Woodward and Chishull agreed, was preaching any millenarian doctrine at all to the untutored. "Consider it as the Case of any single Person," suggested Chishull, "who, if Providentially informed of his Approaching End, immediately becomes useless to the Community in which he lives; he straightway deserts his Calling and his Station, and casts the things of this World behind him. Much more, when the Fate of all things is declared, when the Earth and each inhabitant of the Earth are summoned to an Universal Change, must this needs induce a state of Amazement and Confusion: it must necessarily arrest the whole course of Polity, and put a stop to all the Industry and Ingenuity of Mankind." And if the prophets of the millennium were insincere, it was an easy transition to the deception hypothesis; when men pretended to calculate the end of time, "What else do they endeavour, than, by this Surprise, to Damp the Happy Progress of Arts and Sciences; to Dissolve Societies, to Stop the course of Justice, to Discourage the benefit of Education, and to Extinguish the very Hopes and Prospect of a Posterity."[107] So also the sincere, dizzied by unrelenting attention to prophecies in Scripture, might eventually accept or impose upon many others a vision which ignored the role of the church and the frame of society.

The millenarian critique of the French Prophets concentrated on the social implications of their doctrine and of their behavior as spokesmen for the millennium. Where theologically they might have been but estranged first cousins, Latitudinarian and French Prophet were far more distant relatives in the role they posited for the millenarian. Clerics put the Church and its personnel at the forefront

105. Woodward, *Remarks*, pp. 34, 42–44. Cf. Sir Richard Bulkeley, *An Answer to Several Treatises lately published on the Subject of the Prophets* (1708), pp. 29, 61; John Lacy, *Scene of Delusions . . . Confuted*, p. 44. Although the chronology of judgment was always unclear in the warnings of the French Prophets, they did tend toward a pre-millennial as opposed to post-millennial stance; that is, Jesus would return to initiate the millennium and his Second Coming would take place on a familiar earth at the end of but still within time.

106. Chishull, *Great Danger and Mistake*, p. 16.

107. Ibid., pp. 16–17; cf. Woodward, *Remarks*, p. 28.

of the spiritual work of reformation which would herald the Second Coming; the millenarian minister, chary of the social effects of apocalyptic attitudes, would labor within the body politic to prepare the way for the end. French Prophets argued for less decorous efforts, since in their opinion the Church itself had need of spiritual renewal; the millenarian prophet, eager to embrace new inspiration as a sign and means of renewal, would advance the cause of the Kingdom regardless of some (but by no means all) social conventions. Though churchmen and prophets affirmed identical moral principles and generally advocated a moderate politics, the French Prophets were willing to suspend moral judgment when confronted with the provocative behavior of new self-labeled holy messengers. This willing suspension of judgment, coupled with a personal vision of scriptural prophecy fulfilled at last, was an offense to the "just Reason" of theologians. After a conference with John Lacy and several companions, in which most of the debate concerned behavior rather than doctrine, William Whiston took Lacy by the hand and said, "I hope you are honest, but I am satisfied you are very weak."[108]

Overcome by evil spirits, animal spirits, social effluvia, or by the knotty yet entrancing prophecies of Daniel and St. John, the French Prophets appeared to their enemies as prime examples of human weakness. Whether they succumbed unconsciously to external powers or fostered their own frailty, whether they were innocent and captious fools or sophisticated dreamers and readers of Revelation, the French Prophets threatened the body politic by neglecting the balanced reason which held it together.

The critics of the French Prophets considered behavior in vaguely geometric terms: human action was the resultant of natural forces acting within and without the human frame. Society, like the individual, drew its health from the human capacity to perceive and order those forces. Critics reared or immersed in the late seventeenth-century milieu of medical rationality and Newtonian mechanics, as most were, examined the French Prophets in the light of scientific principles akin to moral precepts: universal stability,

108. William Whiston, *Memoirs* (London, 1749), p. 138.

soul-body harmony. High Churchman and Low Churchman, physician and philosopher adopted the bare speech of common sense to protect society and religion from the unruly and unpredictable. Even John Humfrey, eldest critic, with an enduring attachment to the idea of witchcraft, could lament, "Alas, that a Person of such Reason in Discourse and writing should think that to be transformed into a *Brute* for an Hour or more should be the Way to become a *Prophet*. Oh Mr. Lacy, Mr. Lacy, I am offended and God I think offended, that when his Gracious Spirit descended down on Christ as a Dove, you should be for bringing him down as a Vulture."[109]

109. Humfrey, *Account*, p. 5.

3. Memory

THE FRENCH PROPHETS were sensitive to opposition. In response to theological arguments, they ransacked the Bible as they had never done before and soon began to read widely in Scripture commentaries.[1] In response to criticism of their rude conduct at their own assemblies, they tried to stifle disorders, conscious of themselves as a social unit.[2] Another response in particular demonstrated that the group was well aware of the drift of contemporary theory about human behavior. In order to situate their basic religious experiences within the framework of respectable behavior, they changed their understanding of the process of inspiration.

The *inspirés* in the Cévennes and the first prophets in London had claimed not to remember what they said under ecstasy. They believed that they were passive instruments through which the Lord spoke and that while they prophesied they had no use of their senses. Such a view of the prophetic act protected the inspired from the charge of impurity, of mingling human and divine words.[3] To

1. See Lacy, *The General Delusion of Christians*, pp. 15–16, 468 (where Lacy cites John Locke and Robert Boyle in his defense); Bulkeley, *An Answer to Several Treatises lately published on the Subject of the Prophets*, which exploits the work of the latitudinarian Bishop Stillingfleet (pp. 3, 82), uses William Whiston in defense of the French Prophets (p. 65), and sets Hickes against Edmund Chishull on millennial calculations (pp. 127–28); Misson, *Sentimens désintéressez*, pp. 37, 65, 127, 129, 135, 137, citing Joseph Mede, Stillingfleet, and a passage from the 1681 edition of Hickes's *Spirit of Enthusiasm Exorcised* that was omitted from the 1709 edition.
2. Cf. *English and French Prophets Mad or Bewitcht* [broadside] (1707).
3. *The Devil of Delphos* (1708), p. 109; [Claude Groteste de la Mothe], *Nouveaux*

critics in England, however, lack of memory and loss of reason signified animality and fits of frenzy rather than apostolic gifts. Critics were certain that the apostles had understood what they said, even with the gift of tongues, and that they could recall what they had spoken. If prophets had not the use of their reason and judgment while inspired, how in fact could they personally be assured that their inspiration came from the Lord?[4]

By mid-1707, the French Prophets had adjusted their perception of what occurred under inspiration to include the survival of intellect and memory. Though agitations were involuntary, the prophets were not deprived of their faculties while prophesying. The over-powering Holy Spirit did not render the inspired completely unconscious but left them with mind enough to appreciate the Lord's message.[5] By virtue of this interpretation, the inspired could safely attest to the irresistible force of the Spirit without sacrificing all important human capacities. While able still to deny responsibility for the nature of their prophecies or convulsions, they might free themselves from the implication that they willingly placed themselves in an irrational state. Similarly, manifesting a degree of rationality in the midst of physical turbulence, they might avoid the frequent diagnoses of epilepsy, madness, and other mind-related disorders.[6]

The new emphasis on consciousness, a shift which did not escape the notice of opponents,[7] left its mark on the development of the French Prophets as a millenarian group. Followers had weakened the position of their prophets. The faithful had more cause to fear the confusion of human and divine speech when their prophets were

---

mémoires pour servir à l'histoire des trois Camisars (1708), pp. 21–22; Hoadly, *Brief Vindication of the Antient Prophets*, pp. 34–35. Cf. Lacy, *Relation of Dealings*, p. 15.

4. *Observations upon Elias Marion* (1707), pp. 8–9; N. N., *Account of the Lives and Behaviour of the Three French Prophets* (1708), p. 10; Vernous, *Preservative*, pp. 15–16, 30; Bayly, *An Essay upon Inspiration*, pp. 76, 400; *A Dissuasive Against Enthusiasm* (1708), pp. 46–47.

5. *Clavis Prophetica*, 2:29; *The French Prophet's Declaration* (1707), pp. 2–3; *An Impartial Account of the Prophets In a Letter to a Friend* (1708), p. 15; Lacy, *General Delusion*, p. 10.

6. For rebuttals of these diagnoses or accusations, see *Impartial Account*, pp. 12–15, and Lacy, *General Delusion*, throughout.

7. See *Appeal from the Prophets to their Prophecies* (1708), p. 17; *Reflections on Sir Richard Bulkeley's Answer to Several Treatises* (1708), p. 26; O[swald] E[dwards], *The Shaking-Prophet Alarmed* (Dublin, 1711); Bayly, *An Essay upon Inspiration*, pp. 398–99.

alert during inspiration. The group's nervousness about false prophecy after the failure of Emes's resurrection was aggravated by the changed terms in which the French Prophets described the prophetic act.

The emphasis on consciousness may also have changed the way in which the French Prophets related to one another. When prophets believed that their inspirations happened in the absence of normal awareness, they depended upon an audience to preserve the message and integrity of the inspiration. The prophet was then a social being, though occasionally he or she might receive an internal (unspoken) communication from God; even in that case the prophet's agitations would take place in a group milieu.[8] When the consensus was that prophets were aware of the content of their inspirations, they could begin to assert a degree of independence from their audience. It is striking that the group began to define and expel false prophets only after John Lacy and Sir Richard Bulkeley had begun to reinterpret prophecy as an act during which reasoning and memory continued to function.

Ideas about the coexistence of inspiration and memory may well have conditioned relationships between prophets and followers. More certainly, the act of remembering was vital to the nature of the relationship between the French Prophets and their critics. The French Prophets had a radical, restorative memory. Beyond the act of remembering what one prophesied lay the collective act of remembering a past that had not been experienced—an apostolic past of spiritual intensity. The mixed tenses of the Book of Revelation were a clue to the role and power of memory. What the French Prophets chose to remember most often and most well were a biblical past and future and a prophetic, group-oriented present. Prophecy was a means of creative memory, a re-situation in time. If the prophets at first could not remember their prophecies—if in effect they had suffered from a spiritual timelessness—this could be ascribed to their position as mediators between times. True prophecy was an insight into the "ripeness" of time and a sense of the fusion of all time.[9]

8. See, for example, Marion, *Prophetical Warnings*, pp. 11–22.
9. Cf. the discussion of the role of amnesia in trance in Erika Bourguignon, "The Self, the Behavioral Environment, and the Theory of Spirit Possession," in *Context and Meaning in Cultural Anthropology*, ed. Melford E. Spiro (New York and

For the French Prophets, then, the value of religious ritual was to develop the context for re-situation. Ritual was to be expressive, an acting out of the very process of transformation. Behavior during meetings for worship should consequently be distinctly different from behavior on the street; agitation, convulsions, writhing, and groaning were indices to the behavioral discontinuity implied in prophetic glimpses of other times. When prophecy was not the celebration of past events made immediate, it was the mourning of an event which had not yet occurred. Religious ritual that revolved around prophecy became a ceremony of distended time, so believers were not upset by stuttered inspirations that were highly repetitious and broken by long pauses. The usually slow, reiterative speech of the prophets allowed for careful recording of their words in an environment which promoted a sense of the passage of time wholly distinct from the quotidian. As the group scribes collated the inspirations of the prophets, they provided the French Prophets with another set of memories, the history of the group itself. It was essentially a chronology of the rituals, ordered and official memories of the acts of true recall. Their ritual of prayer, prophecy, and transcription thus had two crucial functions for the French Prophets: it established a context for religious behavior actively expressive of personal transformation, and it helped the group to define itself in the act of remembering its own past.

Critics could admire the apostolic past, and they could encourage the resumption of the values and codes of that time, but they agreed with Lockean logic that it was near madness to integrate that past into one's memory of personal experiences. John Locke had described madness as intellectual anarchy: the mad were unable to distinguish the true data of memory from the fictions of personal fantasy.[10] For their opponents, what the French Prophets called prophecy was not inspired remembrance but misperception, and the

London, 1965), pp. 46–47, 55. See also the important article by J. G. A. Pocock, "Time, History and Eschatology in the Thought of Thomas Hobbes," in *The Diversity of History: Essays in honour of Sir Herbert Butterfield*, ed. J. H. Elliott and H. G. Koenigsberger (Ithaca, 1970), pp. 149–98, esp. p. 179.

10. R. I. Aaron and Jocelyn Gibb, eds., *An Early Draft of Locke's Essay together with Excerpts from his Journals* (Oxford, 1936), p. 104; cf. Locke's *Essay Concerning Human Understanding*, 4th ed. (London, 1700), bk. 2, chap. 11, pars. 12, 13; John R. Clark, *Form and Frenzy in Swift's Tale of a Tub* (Ithaca, 1970), pp. 145–59. For continental theories of memory, see the summaries in Kirkinen, *Les origines de la conception moderne de l'homme machine*, pp. 251, 263, 271, 276, 282.

agitations of the so-called inspired were less likely to be signs of contact with the divine than of physical disorders that underlie misperception.

The critics viewed memory as conservative; memory maintained the proper distance between events, and their proper sequence. To lose one's sense of time was to lose one's reason. The millenarian churchmen and scientists labored privately at the computation of the exact chronology; distances between signal events were divine clues to eschatological mathematics. True prophecy did imply true recall, but inspiration was the gift of interpreting—not eluding—sequence. One stuck fiercely to one's own time (and to the symbolic occurrences of which one was living witness) in order to anchor oneself in the divine schedule. Even if one cherished no hopes of an imminent Second Coming, the conservative accuracy of memory was necessary for a reckoning of God's providences.[11]

For critics, prophecy stood apart from ritual. Ritual, like memory, was conservative; rather than shaping a context for personal transformation, it preserved the integrity of religious traditions. If prophecy entered the realm of worship, it was as prophesying in the Old Testament sense of preaching against moral decline. Ritual time was indistinct from quotidian time, and worshipful behavior in the pew would be consistent with the sober behavior of the good citizen in the street. The ritual milieu was never a privileged space in which religious expression was freed of the normal human duty to maintain an orderly intercourse between citizens. Just as physical interruptions within the body were signs of illness, so behavioral discontinuity was a sign of the loss of memory and the loss of reason.[12]

Most critics, including those who perceived an intrigue behind the

11. On providences, see especially Jacob Viner, *The Role of Providence in the Social Order: An Essay in Intellectual History*, Memoirs of the American Philosophical Society, vol. 90 (Philadelphia, 1972); Thomas, *Religion and the Decline of Magic*, pp. 78–112, 639–40; Aubrey Williams, "Interpositions of Providence and the Design of Fielding's Novels," *South Atlantic Quarterly* 70 (Spring 1971):265–86.

12. Cf. Victor Turner, "Passages, Margins, and Poverty: Religious Symbols of Communitas," in his *Dramas, Fields, and Metaphors: Symbolic Action in Human Society* (Ithaca and London, 1974), pp. 231–71; Mary Douglas, *Natural Symbols: Explorations in Cosmology* (New York, 1973 [1970]), pp. 19–39. Both make thoughtful, imaginative contributions toward an understanding of ritual time and ritual space. See also Mircea Eliade, *Cosmos and History: The Myth of the Eternal Return*, trans. W. R. Trask (New York, 1959 [1949]).

dancing display of prophecy and miracle, assumed that the majority of French Prophets were unable to organize their experience properly. What believers identified as miracles, for example, were either actions for which there is a physical explanation that relies upon the existence of invisible but material substances, or actions for which we have no explanation yet but which have counterparts in nonreligious contexts, such as the fantastic strength and endurance of mad people. However deeply miracle and prophecy were imbedded in the foundation of Christian faith, they had their reality within the social memory of the Church as a bearer of tradition, not within personal experience. Somehow the French Prophets had confused memory and experience; they had understood Scripture miracles as models for new miracles rather than as unique proofs of Christianity furnished by the Lord during the first centuries of the spread of the true religion. First the French Prophets mistook their own historical placement, then they mistook the significance of their own feelings and of events around them. It followed that they would behave inappropriately. It also followed that their agitations—which they thought to be analogous to personal religious transformation—were the result of physical disturbances that came out of a misalignment of body and soul. The assemblies of the French Prophets gave weak people the opportunity to admire their own weakness, to glory in confusion.

The act of prophecy confronted eighteenth-century men and women with problems that were as much physical as they were religious. Critics of the French Prophets who had been reared in an atmosphere of Cartesian and then Newtonian mechanics wanted desperately to explain the behavior of false prophets in terms of natural forces operating within and through the body, just as the natural philosophers of the late seventeenth century hoped to establish philosophy upon the bedrock of chemical or physical interactions. The medical world, whether iatrochemical or iatrophysical, relied upon subtle particles called animal spirits as the medium through which the soul became physically operative; the new physics and chemistry often relied upon certain invisible substances known as aether and effluvia as the mediums in which natural forces—gravitational, magnetic, electric—might move. Scientist-physicians rephrased the religious questions about miracle and prophecy in material terms: can forces act at a distance, or must all forces be transmitted through the contact of bodies? The prophets, of course, knew that the original, immediate source of their inspirations was the Holy Spirit or, at the very least, an angelic messenger; they were claiming that in 1707, in London, the spiritual world did act at a distance upon the physical world in obvious and dramatic ways. The opponents chose to debate the spiritual-physical interaction itself. They did not simply discourse on the nature of the spirits which moved the French Prophets. They discredited the prophets by reducing all inexplicable behavior to the results of natural, physical, but possibly hidden interactions.

As Sir Richard Bulkeley had guessed, the French Prophets were caught in a historical trap. Although no critic was willing to deny the possibility of divine inspiration and no critic proposed a wholly mechanical explanation of human behavior, most critics pressed for an understanding of human activity based upon the interaction of natural forces. The greater their success in penetrating to the laws governing natural forces, the less likely they would be to acknowledge mysterious human actions as evidence of supernatural forces, demonic or divine. Remarkable cures, speaking in tongues, and levitation were rather provocative instances for which there were precedents but no sufficient material explanations. Inexplicable behavior was no evidence of supernatural intervention; rather it revealed the insufficiency of present knowledge.

Aether, animal spirits, and effluvia were contemporary hypotheses invented to sustain physicalist explanations of the behavior of natural phenomena. Almost always critics appealed to natural forces and invisible mediums whose operation ensured that action at a distance—though possible for the divine—was not in play with the French Prophets. Critics made use of animal spirits and of a series of metaphors which extended animal spirits beyond the individual to the body politic: imagination, enthusiasm, contagion. Eliminating supernatural forces from the sphere of contemporary human activity, critics could put all individual behavior within the purview of physiology and all social behavior within the purview of politics. Religious behavior *was* explicable in the same manner as all other human behavior, and the same system of forces articulated within the body could by extension apply to the social context of religion.

In the range of attitudes from oldest to youngest critic, what was shifting was not confidence in human rationality so much as the understanding of the relationship between reason and emotion. The possession hypothesis implied that the strongest emotions and the largest gestures were in a realm entirely separate from reason. Physical hyperbole, inverted or disconcerting discourse were not human at all but otherworldly. The medical hypothesis of animal spirits began to link emotions to reason on the inner geography of the human body. The hypothesis of enthusiasm and effluvia made it clear that thoughts had emotional repercussions and that somehow groups of people might share emotional currents. Critics and prophets both recognized an equivalence between motion and emotion. For the critics, straining in a physical universe newly bounded by Newtonian laws, in a social universe at stress under commercial expansion, in a political universe which still tilted if it no longer overturned, motion and emotion had to have their paths carefully plotted. [13]

Critics desired to regulate religious emotions as motion itself could be regulated in the physical universe. They allowed little leeway for the outward expression of religious feelings. The restraint on religious sensation was rooted in scientific, social, and theological observations: medical theory proposed that strong emotions of any sort are the results of chemical upset or mechanical interference within the human body; the social theory of contagion held that powerful religious emotions are most likely to be transmitted through the imagination and its accompanying harmful effluvia; the religious history of England in the preceding century argued persuasively for a steady and inevitable association among overstrong religious feelings, enthusiasm, and fanaticism. Now that reason and passion were seen to be hooked to one another within the human frame, reason had to supply that equilibrium of the self by which attractive and repulsive forces worked in harmony.

But what forces determine behavior? The theory of human behavior refined by the critics of the French Prophets offered no satisfying answer. Critics supposed that human behavior was governed by natural forces acting within—not on—the person or the group. The analogy from physics to physiology held good, and

---

13. Cf. J. H. Plumb, "Reason and Unreason in the Eighteenth Century: The English Experience," in *Some Aspects of Eighteenth-Century England. Papers read at a Clark Library Seminar, March 7, 1970* (Berkeley and Los Angeles, 1971), pp. 6–12; Hill, *Change and Continuity in Seventeenth-Century England*, on "Reason" and "Reasonableness," pp. 103–23; Michel Foucault, *Folie et déraison* (Paris, 1961); Bertrand H. Bronson, "The Retreat from Reason," in *Irrationalism in the Eighteenth Century*, ed. Harold E. Pagliaro (Cleveland, 1972), pp. 225–38.

motion within the person or group was subject to the principle of inertia. Behavior was not manipulable from a distance without a communicating medium; reason, the passions, and the nerves made physical contact with one another. Changes in human behavior had immediately to do with the state of the communicating mediums within the body or between people. The communicating mediums were so configured as to be peculiarly adapted to the variety of tasks assigned to them; animal spirits, for example, were thought to be fine particles akin to spirit of wine and moving like a fluid—in other words, they shared the qualities of solids, liquids, and gases. Only by such virtuosity of character could they communicate with muscles, animal juices, air, and the soul.

Where in all of this was the human *being*? Was there something more to life than motion? The eighteenth-century vitalist physician Georg Ernst Stahl suspected that each living body contained an active principle (*ens*) and an immanent force (*anima*); his views would later inform the development of biological theory. Eighteenth-century English natural philosophers would assume that forces were present within bodies, and this assumption would determine the direction of much chemical and physical experimentation.[14] The answer of William Law and the Wesleys was to

14. On medicine, see King, "Rationalism in Early Eighteenth Century Medicine," and "Stahl and Hoffman: A Study in Eighteenth Century Animism"; Elizabeth L. Haigh, "Vitalism, The Soul, and Sensibility: The Physiology of Théophile Bordeu," *Journal of the History of Medicine* 31 (1976):30–41. On natural philosophy and chemistry, see F. F. Centore, "Mechanism, Teleology, and Seventeenth Century English Science," *International Philosophical Quarterly* 12 (1972):553–71; Thackray, *Atoms and Powers: An Essay on Newtonian Matter-Theory and the Development of Chemistry*, pp. 129–31, 145–46, and throughout; Robert E. Schofield, *Mechanism and Materialism: British Natural Philosophy in an Age of Reason* (Princeton, 1970), esp. pp. 91–93; Jammer, *Concepts of Force: A Study in the Foundations of Dynamics*, pp. 158–215; P. M. Heimann and J. E. McGuire, "Newtonian Forces and Lockean Powers: Concepts of Matter in Eighteenth-Century Thought," in *Historical Studies in the Physical Sciences* 3 (1971):233–306. In their complex article, Heimann and McGuire describe a transition from beliefs in "active principle" to beliefs in "active substance" in eighteenth-century natural philosophy. They would argue, I suspect, that my analogy between aether and animal spirits as mediums of communication is simplistic. They hold that Newton saw that forces do act at a distance in nature, and that Newton had employed the concept of aether "to establish God's causal connection with nature," a concept which eighteenth-century scientists transformed "to support a theory of the balance of nature, a view which conceived nature as a self-contained system independent of divine intervention" (p. 236). I am arguing that the critics of the French Prophets, in their zeal to impugn all violent "religious" behavior, cut away many of the implicitly religious aspects of the concepts of aether, animal spirits, and effluvia. Like Newton's aether, the concept of animal spirits may

call for vital religion; emotions within the self were a kind of spiritual force.[15]

The turn inward which characterized early eighteenth-century English piety may have been part of a move—recognizable in physiological animism and vitalism and in basic ideas about the location of forces in space—toward the reassertion of a spiritual (immaterial) component in all behavior. The critics of the French Prophets had so completely restricted valid religious expression that there was little distinction between everyday activity and worship.[16] What had lost its power was ritual, something the French Prophets took most seriously and so shocked their English audiences. In the Cévennes, "Desert" rituals had been potent because they were the carriers of a group memory in the absence of chapels and books. Camisard ritual had combined prophecy and prayer, anticipation and memory, sign and force. In England, the *inspirés* and their followers hoped to preserve this religious excitement about events, but their critics attacked their willful confusion of memory and experience, their physical abandonment freely expressive of religious transformation. The response to the dilemma of worship into which the critics had inadvertently put all of Christianity was,

have been advocated apart from mechanistic theory, but the critics, in refusing to acknowledge any true inspiration or possession among the French Prophets, confined the role of animal spirits to the mechanical and natural.

15. On the bases for the Methodist revival, see John Walsh, "The Origins of the Evangelical Revival," *Essays in Modern English Church History*, ed. G. V. Bennett and John D. Walsh (London, 1966), pp. 132–62; Donald Davie, "Old Dissent, 1700–1740," *Times Literary Supplement*, Nov. 26, 1976, pp. 1491–92. On criticisms of the Methodists similar to those of the French Prophets, see John Walsh, "Methodism and the Mob in the Eighteenth Century," in *Popular Belief and Practice*, Studies in Church History, vol. 8, ed. G. J. Cuming and Derek Baker (Cambridge, 1972), pp. 213–28; Arthur P. Whitney, *The Basis of Opposition to Methodism in England in the Eighteenth Century* (New York, 1951). When the Methodists appeared, some critics explicitly recalled the French Prophets as part of their attack on Wesleyan revivals: Anti-Enthusiasticus, *The Wonderful Narrative: Or, a Faithful Account of the French Prophets, their Agitations, Exstasies, and Inspirations* (Glasgow, 1742); George W. Lavington, *The Enthusiasm of Methodists and Papists Compared*, 2d ed., 2 parts (London, 1749), 2:72; James Robe, *A Faithful Narrative of the Extraordinary Work of God, at Kilsyth* (Glasgow, 1742), pp. 52–54 (on the campaign of opponents to identify the revival with the French Prophets' agitations). Cf. E. S. Gaustad, "Charles Chauncey and the Great Awakening: A Survey and Bibliography," *Papers of the Bibliographical Society of America* 45 (1951):125–35; Jonathan Edwards, *Some Thoughts Concerning the present Revival of Religion in New-England*, ed. C. G. Goen (New Haven, 1972 [1742]), pp. 313, 330, 341. In a future work I will deal at some length with the contacts between the French Prophets and early Methodists.

16. Cf. Russell E. Richey, "Effects of Toleration on Eighteenth-Century Dissent," *Journal of Religious History* 8 (1975):350–63.

for some, a renewal of the inner, hardly visible spiritual life. The manuals of piety, the quietist letters and pietist books, the Moravian lectures and Methodist sermons began often enough with instruction in a particular method: how to identify those faint internal expressions of the spirit. The appeal of the evangelical revival of the 1740s may have been due in part to a desire to restore integrity to expansive, expressive, outwardly religious behavior.

Appendix: Profiles of Opponents, 1707–10

Name	DOB	Religion	Position	Hypotheses
John Humfrey	1621	Congregationalist	Rector, London	All
Edward Fowler	1632	C. of E., Broad Church	Bishop of Gloucester	Demon and enthusiasm
Richard Kingston	ca. 1635	C. of E.	Rector, Suffolk, but not ordained?	All
Marc Vernous	1635	Huguenot [Mazamet]	Pastor, London	Disease and enthusiasm
Jean Blanc	1640	Huguenot	Pastor, London	Imposture
George Hickes	1642	High Church nonjuror	Nonjuring bishop	Delusion
Jean Graverol	1647	Huguenot	Pastor, London	Imposture
Claude Groteste de la Mothe	1647	Huguenot [Paris]	Minister, Savoy Church, London	Disease and delusion
Robert Calder	1650	Scottish Episcopalian	Minister, Edinburgh	Delusion
Thomas Morer	1652	C. of E.	Rector, London	Delusion
Nathaniel Spinckes	1653	High Church nonjuror	Chaplain to Duke of Lauderdale	Demon and delusion
Thomas d'Urfey*	1653	C. of E.(?)	Writer	Imposture
Offspring Blackall	1654	C. of E., High Church	Bishop of Exeter	Enthusiasm
Josiah Woodward	1656?	C. of E., Broad Church	Minister, Poplar	All
James Hog	1658	Scottish Presbyterian	Minister, Carnock	Delusion and enthusiasm

Name	Year	Religious affiliation	Occupation	Attitude
Daniel Defoe	1660	Dissenter	Writer	Delusion
Francis Hutchinson	1660	C. of E., Broad Church	Curate, Suffolk	Delusion and disease
Edmund Calamy*	1661	Moderate Presbyterian	Minister, Westminster	Delusion
William King*	1663	C. of E.	Writer	Enthusiasm and imposture
William Whiston	1667	C. of E., but Arian and Broad Church	Prof. of mathematics, Cambridge (exp. 1711)	Delusion
Pierre Rival	ca. 1670	Huguenot [Saliès]	Minister, Artillery Church, London	**
Benjamin Bayly	1671	C. of E.	Rector, Bristol	Enthusiasm and disease
Edmund Chishull	1671	C. of E., Broad Church?	Minister, Essex	Enthusiasm and delusion
Anthony Ashley Cooper, 3d earl of Shaftes-bury	1671	Deist	M.P., House of Lords	Enthusiasm
Benjamin Hoadly	1676	C. of E., Broad Church	Rector, London	Delusion
Henry Nicholson	1683?	C. of E.; apostate French Prophet	Student; physician?	Delusion and disease

*Had Huguenot ancestry.

**Only extant published work is directed exclusively against Huguenot minister Jean Lions, a sympathizer with the French Prophets.

NOTES: For Huguenots, their French origins rather than religious stance are listed, since their attitude toward the *inspirés* was determined in part by their familiarity with southeastern France.

This appendix includes only those opponents who published articles, tracts, or books against the French Prophets between 1707 and 1710. Other active opponents who did not publish or who published with successful anonymity were John Chamberlayne (b. 1666), gentleman of the bedchamber to Queen Anne, and Pierre Testas (b. ca. 1654), Huguenot pastor in London, originally from Milhau.

The Opposition to the French Prophets:
Bibliography of Primary Works

All works are located in the British Museum unless otherwise noted.

1. Opposition Broadsides, Tracts and Pamphlets, 1706–10

Account of the Apprehending and Taking Six French Prophets, Near Hog-Lane in Soho, who pretended to Prophecy that the World should be at an End within this three weeks, with several other ridiculous Prognostications; with the manner of their Examination and Binding Over, on Monday the 28th of April, by Several Justices of Peace sitting on St. Martins Vestry: As also an Account of the Examination and Binding Over above 20 French People more, for beating and assaulting the Worshipful Justice, for faithfully executing the Duty of his Office. Broadside. London, 1707. Copy at Bodleian Library, Oxford.

An Account of the Pretended Prophets, newly come from England, and their Doctrine briefly Considered. Edinburgh (?), 1709. Copy at Houghton Library, Harvard University.

An Account of the Tryal, Examination and Conviction, of Elias Marion, and other French Prophets, at the Queen's-Bench Bar, the 4th of July, 1707. at Guild-Hall, before the right Honourable the Lord Chief Justice Holt; for publishing False and Scandalous Pamphlets; and gathering Tumultuous Assemblies. Broadside. London, 1707.

Account of the Tryal, Examination and Conviction of the Pretended French Prophets, At the Queen's-Bench Bar at Guild-Hall, this Day, being Friday the 4th of July, 1707. London, 1707. Copy at Bodleian Library, Oxford.

An Appeal from the Prophets to their Prophecies. Evidencing the new Dispensation they pretend, to be of the same Stamp and Authority with their Predictions. London, 1708.

Bayly, Benjamin. *An Essay upon Inspiration. In Two Parts.* 2d ed., corrected and enlarged. London, 1708.

Blackall, Offspring. *"The Way of Trying Prophets": A Sermon Preached before the Queen at St. James's, November 9, 1707.* London, 1707, 2d and 3d eds., 1707, 4th ed., 1709. Translated into French as *"La manière d'examiner les prophètes" Sermon prononcé devant la REINE.*London,1708. Copy of the French ed. at the Library of the French Protestant Church, Soho, London.

Blanc, Jean. *L'anathème des faux prophètes. Sermon prononcé dans les Eglises Françoises de l'Artillerie, de Leicesterfields, de Ridercourt et du Tabernacle.* London, 1707. Copy at National Library of Scotland, Edinburgh. Translated into English as *The Anathema of the False Prophets in a Sermon Preached in several French Churches in and about London.* London, 1708. Copies at Library of Huguenot Society of London and at University of Texas.

Calamy, Edmund. *A Caveat against New Prophets, in Two Sermons [on Jer. xiv. 14] at the Merchants Lecture in Salters Hall, on Jan. the 6th and Jan. the 20th, 1707/8.* London, 1708.

————. *Sir Richard Bulkeley's Remarks on the Caveat against New Prophets Considered, in a Letter to a Friend.* London, 1708.

Calder, Robert. *A True Copy of Letters Past betwixt Mr. Robert Calder Minister of the Gospel, and Mr. James Cuninghame of Barns, Concerning the Trial of the Mission of these People, that pass under the Name of Prophets, In Scotland and England, with A Relation of the failing of their Prophecies, and the True Character of an Enthusiast.* Edinburgh, 1710.

Chishull, Edmund. *The Great Danger and Mistake Of all New Uninspired Prophecies, Relating to the End of the World. Being a Sermon Preached on Nov. 23rd, 1707. At Serjeants-Inn-Chappel, in Chancery-Lane.* London, 1708.

Clavis Prophetica; or, a Key to the Prophecies of Mons. Marion, and the other Camisars, With some Reflections on the Characters of these New Envoys, and of Mons. F. their Chief Secretary. 2 parts. London, 1707. Translated into French in 1708(?), but I have not located a copy of the French edition.

[Collett, Mr.] *The Honnest Quaker, or, The Forgeries and Impostures Of the Pretended French Prophets and their Abettors Exposed, in a Letter from a Quaker to his Friend, Giving an Account of a Sham-Miracle Performed by John L[ac]y Esq on the Body of Elizabeth Gray, on the 17th of August last.* London, 1707. Reprinted in 1711 as *A Quaker, The Imposture Detected: Or, the Modern French Prophets, Exemplified.* Copy of the reprint at Friends' House Library, London.

The Devil of Delphos, or The Prophets of Baal: containing an Account of a Notorious Impostor, called Sabatai Sevi, pretended Messiah of the Jews, in 1666. Who afterwards turned Turk: And of many other Impostors in Church and State; as, False Christs, and False Prophets from the Rise of Christianity to the Present Times. To which is added, A Proof that the Present Pretended Prophets are the Prophets of the Devil, and not of God. London, 1708.

A Dissuasive against Enthusiasm: Wherein the Pretensions of the Modern Prophets to Divine Inspiration, and the Power of Working Miracles, are examined and confuted by Scripture and Matter of Fact. London, 1708.

The English and French Prophets Mad or Bewitcht, At their Assemblies in Baldwins Gardens, on Wednesday the 12th of November, at Four of the Clock in the Afternoon, and Thursday the 13th, and on Sunday the 16th, at Barbican, With an Account of their Tryal, 1707. Broadside. London, 1707. Reprinted, abbreviated, in pamphlet form: *The French Prophets Mad Sermon, As Preacht since their Sufferings at their several Assemblies held in Baldwins-Gardens, at Barbican, Pancras-Wells, and several other Places in and about London. Done into French and English.* London, 1708.

An Epitaph on the French Prophet, Who was to make his Resurrection the 25th of May. Another on the same Prophet: Written by himself. Edinburgh, 1709. Copy at National Library of Scotland, Edinburgh.

The French Prophetess turned Adamite. Being a True and Comical Account of a Pretended French Prophetess, who on Sunday the 16th of November, did in a very Immodest and Indecent manner (being inspired with a pretended Spirit) undress herself stark Naked at the Popish Chapel in Lincoln's-Inn Fields, and forced her self through the Crowd up to the Altar, in order to preach her new doctrine. London, 1707(?). Reprinted by W. Sparrow Simpson in "Lincoln's Inn Fields: The French Prophetess," *Notes and Queries*, 6th ser., 11, no. 263 (Jan. 10, 1885): 21–22.

The French Prophet's Declarations; or An Account of the Preachings, Prophecies and Warnings of Elias Marion, One of the Chief of the Pretended Inspired Protestant Prophets, and others of them; at their Meeting-House in Barbican, as they were uttered by the operation of the Spirit: Foretelling of many strange and wonderful things that shall shortly come to pass. London, 1707.

The French Prophet's Resurrection: With his Speech to the Multitude that behold the MIRACLE. Broadside. London, 1708. Copy at Library of Huguenot Society of London.

Graverol, Jean. *Réflexions désinteressées sur certains pretendus inspirez, qui, depuis quelques temps, se mêlent de prophetiser dans Londres.* 2 parts. London, 1707. Copy at the Library of the French Protestant Church, Soho, London.

Hickes, George. *The Spirit of Enthusiasm Exorcised: in a Sermon Preached before the University of Oxford, on Act-Sunday, July 11, 1680.* 4th ed., much enlarged. London, 1709.

Hog, James. *Notes about The Spirit's Operations, For discovering from the Words, their Nature and Evidence. Together with Diverse Remarks for Detecting the Enthusiastical Delusions of the Cevennois, Antonia Bourignon, and Others.* 2d ed. Edinburgh, 1709.

Humfrey, John. *An Account of the French Prophets, And their Pretended Inspirations, in Three Letters sent to John Lacy, Esq; By one that is concerned for his Friend: A Lover of Truth, and a Hater of Persecution.* London, 1708. First letter also printed separately in broadside: a Lover of Verity, a Hater of Persecution. *A Warning concerning the French Prophets: Being Advice for those that go after them to take heed lest they fall into Fits, as they do, and others have done, by often seeing and continuing among them.* London, 1707.

———. *A Farther Account of our Late Prophets, in Two Letters to Sir Richard Buckley, which May be added to the Three sent to Mr. Lacy.* London, 1708.

Hutchinson, Francis. *A Short View of the Pretended Spirit of Prophecy, Taken from its First Rise in the Year 1688, To its Present State among us.* London, 1708.

Keith, George. *The Magick of Quakerism or, the Chief Mysteries of Quakerism Laid Open. To which are added, A Preface and Postscript relating to the Camisars, in answer to Mr. Lacy's Preface to the Cry from the Desart.* London, 1707.

[King, William]. *The Prophets: an Heroic Poem. In 3 Cantos, Humbly Inscribed to the Illumined Assembly at Barbican.* London, 1708.

Kingston, Richard. *Enthusiastick Impostors No Divinely Inspired Prophets.* 2 parts. London, 1707, 1709.

A Lay-Gentleman [Francis Lee]. *The History of Montanism.* London, 1709.

Le Sage, George-Louis. *L'examen des esprits, ou, essay sur les caracteres d'une vocation divine, dans un sermon à l'imitation de celui du Docteur Blackall, sur le même texte.* London, 1708. Reprinted in Amsterdam, 1721. Copies of both at B.P.U.G.

A Letter from Dr. Emes to the MOB, Assembled at his Grave, Discovering the True Design of the Prophesie relating to his Resurrection, as he Transcribed it from the Minutes taken in Hell by the Juncto that sat upon that Affair. London, 1708(?). Copy at Library of Huguenot Society of London.

M---m, A----r. *An Account of a Dream at Harwich, In a Letter to a Member of Parliament about the Camisars.* London, 1708.

———. *An Account of a Dream at Harwich, Supplying all the Omissions and Defects of the First Dream.* London, 1709.

Merlin. *Ancienne prediction du celebre prophete Merlin. Copiée sur une traduction en vieux Gaulois, qui en fut faite sous le regne d'Henry VIII.* London(?), 1708(?). Includes *Nouvelle prophetie d'Elie Marion, N.F. J.D. et C.P. tenant la plume. Fidellement transcrite et maintenant publiée par l'auteur du premier dialogue touchant les prophetes cevennois. Du dimanche 25 may.* Also includes *La magie blanche, ou les trois prophetes cevennois.* See entry under Rémy.

Mesnard, Philippe. *Les faux prophetes convaincus. Quatre sermons sur S. Mat. Ch. VII ver 15.16. Prononcez dans la Chapelle Royale Françoise du Palais de St. James.* London, 1708. Copy at B.P.U.G.

The mighty Miracle; or The Wonder of Wonders at Windmill Hill. London, 1708. Reprinted in vol. 7 of *The Harleian Miscellany,* edited by William Oldys and Thomas Park. 12 vols. London, 1808–11.

Morer, Thomas. *Sermons on Several Occasions. . . . One concerning Agitations.* London, 1708.

Mothe, Claude Groteste de la. *Caractere des nouvelles prophecies. En quatre sermons prononcez dans l'Eglise Françoise de la Savoye.* London, 1708.

———. *Examen du théâtre sacré des Cévennes.* London, 1708.

———. *Nouveaux memoires pour servir à l'histoire des trois Camisars, ou l'on voit les declarations de Monsieur le Colonel Cavalier, etc.* London, 1708.

———. *Relation de ce qui s'est passé sur l'affaire du Sieur Jean Lions Ministre: Et du jugement qui en a été fait le 15 octob. 1707 dans l'Assemblée Générale des trois consistoires dont il dépend.* London, 1707. Copy at the library of the French Protestant Church, Soho, London.

N., N. *An Account of the Lives and Behaviour of the Three French Prophets Lately come out of the Cevennes and Languedoc; And of the Proceedings of the Consistory of the Savoy in Relation to them.* Part 1 (no second part published?). London, 1708.

Nicholson, Henry. *The Falsehood of the New Prophets Manifested with their Corrupt Doctrines and Conversations By one who hath had intimate Conversation with them, whilst he had an Opinion of their Integrity: But now thinks himself obliged to discover their Enormities, for the Publick Benefit.* London, 1708.

Observations upon Elias Marion, and his Book of Warnings, Lately Published, Proving this Elias to be a false Prophet, and a dangerous Person. London, 1707.

P., G. *The Shortest Way with the French Prophets. Or, an Impartial Relation of the Rise, Progress, and Total Suppression of those Seducers who attempted lately to Pervert several Inhabitants in the Town of Birmingham in Warwickshire. . . . To which is added a Letter from John Lacy Esq: to his new Friend there.* London, 1708.

Un Particulier. *Lettres à Monsieur Misson, l'honnête homme.* London, 1707–8.

A Person of Honour. *A Confutation of the Prophets: or, Mr. Lacy brought to a Right Understanding.* London, 1708. Copies at Cambridge University and at the University of Texas.

Philadelphus, G. *An Answer* [to Francis Moult's *The Right Way of Trying Prophets,* added] *thereunto, Paragraph by Paragraph, Together with Some Remarks on the Knowledge of the DEVIL in Contingent Futurities, and Natural Philosophy; as delivered in a Sermon, November 9, 1707.* London, 1708.

Pillory Disappointed, or the False Prophets Advancement. To the Tune of Rotten Eggs, Turnop-Tops, Pieces of Dirt, and Brick Batts. Broadside. London, 1707. Copy at Bodleian Library, Oxford.

Reflections on Sir Richard Bulkeley's Answer to Several Treatises Lately published, on the Subject of the Prophets. London, 1708.

[Rémy, Clement]. *Sept dialogues entre deux frères touchant les prophetes cevenois.* London(?), 1707. Copy at Bodleian Library, Oxford.

A Reply to the main Argument In a Paper, Entituled, An Impartial Account of the Prophets, in a Letter to a Friend. London, 1708.

[Rival, Pierre]. *Refutation de la pretendue apologie, du Sieur Lions Ministre suspendu à l'occasion des faux prophetes.* Part 1 (no second part published?). London(?), 1708(?). Title page missing from only known copy, Library of the French Protestant Church, Soho, London.

Satyrical Reflection on the Vices and Follies of the Age. Containing, I. A Satyr on the French Prophets. . . . First of at least seven parts, the seventh part entitled Reflections, Moral, Comical, Satyrical, etc. On the Vices and Follies of the Age. Containing, . . . XIV. An Epitaph on Dr. Emmes. London, 1707–8.

Spinckes, Nathaniel. *The New Pretenders to Prophecy Examined, and Their Pretences Shewn to be Groundless and False.* London, 1709.

—–—. *The New Pretenders to Prophecy Re-examined.* London, 1710.

Tryal, Examination, and Condemnation of the French Prophets, Who were Sentenced on Friday the 26th of November, at the Queen's-Bench-Bar at Westminster, for holding several unlawful Assemblies, contrary to the Laws and Customs of this Kingdom. London, 1707. Copy at Bodleian Library, Oxford.

Urfey, Thomas d'. *The Modern Prophets: or, New Wit for a Husband.* London, 1709. The music for the songs in this satirical play appears in d'Urfey's *Songs Compleat, Pleasant and Divertive; set to Musick By Dr. John Blow, Mr. Henry Purcell, and other Excellent Masters of the Town.* 2 vols. London, 1719.

Vernous, Mark [Marc]. *A Preservative Against the False Prophets of the Times: Or, A Treatise Concerning True and False Prophets, With their Characters: Likewise A Letter to Mr. Maximilian Misson, upon the Subject of the Miracles, pretended to be wrought by the French Prophets, and their Adherents.* London, 1708.

Whiston, William. *The Accomplishment of Scripture Prophecies. Being Eight Sermons Preached at the Cathedral Church of St. Paul, in the Year MDCCVII. At the Lecture Founded by the Honourable Robert Boyle Esq; With an Appendix.* Cambridge, 1708.

Whitehead, George. *Power of Christ Vindicated, Against the Magick of Apostasy: In Answer to George Keith's Book, Abusively Stiled, The Magick of Quakerism.* London, 1708.

Woodward, Josiah. *An Answer to the Letter of John Lacy, Esq; Dated July 6, 1708. And Directed to Josiah Woodward, D.D.* London, 1708.

—–—. *The Copy of a Letter to Mr. F[rancis] M[oult]. A Gentleman, Who is a Follower of the Pretended Prophets. Shewing the Reasons why they ought to be accounted Impostors.* London, 1708.

—–—. *Remarks on the Modern Prophets, And on some Arguments Lately published in their Defense.* London, 1708.

2. Later Opposition Works

Anderson, John. *A Defence of the Church Government, Faith, Worship and Spirit of the Presbyterians.* Glasgow, 1714.

Anti-Enthusiasticus. *The Wonderful Narrative: Or, a Faithful Account of the French Prophets, their Agitations, Extasies, and Inspirations.* Glasgow, 1742.

E[dwards], O[swald]. *The Shaking-Prophets alarmed, In beholding a lighted Candle, Taken from God's Sanctuary; or A Beacon Fired on the top of an Hill to Give Men light in the Night of Time.* Dublin, 1711. Copy at Bodleian Library, Oxford.

Keimer, Samuel. *Brand pluck'd from the Burning: Exemplifyed in the Unparalleled CASE of Samuel Keimer, Offered to the Perusal of the Serious Part of Mankind, and especially to those who were ever acquainted with, or ever heard of the Man.* London, 1718.

———. *The Platonick Courtship. A Poem.* London, 1718. Copy held by Library Company of Philadelphia.

———. *A Search after Religion, Among the many Modern Pretenders to it. . . . To which is added, An address and Petition to King Jesus.* London, 1716 or later.

Rhind, Thomas. *An Apology.* Edinburgh, 1712.

Note: All continental publications against the French Prophets have been omitted from this bibliography.

3. Controversial Writings by the French Prophets

Bulkeley, Sir Richard, 2d Baronet. *An Answer to Several Treatises lately published on the Subject of the Prophets. The First Part.* London, 1708. The next entry is the second part.

———. *Preface to the Reader of Warnings of the Eternal Spirit, Spoken by the Mouth of the Servant of God, Abraham Whitro.* London, 1709.

An Impartial Account of the Prophets in a Letter to a Friend. London, 1708. 2d and 3d eds., London, 1708, an Edinburgh printing, 1708. Translated into French as *Relation sans partialité, touchant les prophètes, dans un lettre à un ami* and appended to the French translation of John Lacy's *Warnings.* (1707). Reprint of 1st ed. in 1795. Copy of French edition at Wellcome Medical Historical Library, London.

Jackson, James. *An Appeal to Country Friends at this General Yearly Meeting: Shewing the Unchristian Carriage of some City Friends to such as are taught of God, under the present Dispensation of the Spirits Ministry. And a Copy of their Excommunicating Process for the Same. With Animadversions thereon.* London, 1708.

———. *The Great Question Answered; Viz. Whether the Warnings by the Mouth of John, Sirnamed Lacy, etc. be of God, or from Delusion? With Cautionary Advice Thereon.* London, 1707.

Lacy, John. *Esquire Lacy's Reasons why Doctor Emes was not raised from the Dead.* London, 1708. Reprinted in vol. 7 of *The Harleian Miscellany,* edited by William Oldys and Thomas Park. 12 vols. London, 1808–11.

———. *The General Delusion of Christians, Touching the Ways of God's revealing Himself, To, and By the Prophets, Evinced from Scripture and Primitive Antiquity. And many Principles of Scoffers, Atheists, Sadducees and Wild Enthusiasts, refuted. The Whole adapted, as much as possible, to the meanest Capacity.* London, 1713.

———. *Mr. Lacy's Letter to the Reverend Dr. Josiah Woodward, Concerning his Remarks on the Modern Prophets.* London, 1708.

———. *A Relation of the Dealings of God to his Unworthy Servant John Lacy, Since the Time of his Believing and Professing himself Inspired.* London, 1708.

———. *The Scene of Delusions, By the Reverend Mr. Owen of Warrington, At his own Earnest Request, Considered and Confuted, By One of the Modern Prophets; and (as it proves) partly by Himself.* London, [1723].

Lions, Jean. *Apologie de Jean Lions Ministre, avec des réflexions sur les écrits des Sieurs Pégorier, Lamote, et Rival.* London, 1708.

———. *Relation de ce qui s'est passé entre Jean Lions ministre et les consistoires.* London, 1707. Copy at B.P.U.G.

Misson, François-Maximilien. *Meslange de literature historique et critique sur tout ce qui regarde l'etat extraordinaire des Cevennois, appellez Camisards.* London, 1707.

———. *Le nouvel hosanna des petits enfans. Ou, relation des assemblées saintes, et admirables, qui font presque tous les enfans, dans la Silésie, pour adorer Dieu.* (Translation of a letter published in Bulkeley's *Answer to Several Treatises,* and including also a translation and comment upon Offspring Blackall's *The Way of Trying Prophets.*) London, 1708. Copy at B.P.U.G.

———. *Plainte et censure des calomnieuses accusations publiées par le Sr. Claude Groteste de la Motte, contre ceux qui ont reçu les dépositions du Théâtre sacré des Cévennes.* London, 1708.

———. *Réflexions apologétiques de l'auteur du Mélange de litérature etc. sur un certain rapport scandaleux, frauduleusement fait au L. E[vêque] d'Exeter.* London. 1708. Copy at B.P.U.G.

———. *Sentimens désinteressez de divers théologiens protestans sur les agitations et sur les autres particularités de l'état des prophètes.* London, 1708.

M[oult], F[rancis]. *The Right Way of Trying Prophets: Or, Some Considerations and Reasons to Prove the Truth of the great Dispensation of Divine Providence; already begun by Prophetic Inspiration: To wit, The sudden Appearance of the Kingdom of Christ upon Earth, by the wonderful Effusion of the Holy Ghost.* London, 1707 or 1708.

Pickworth, Henry. *A Charge of Error, Heresy, Incharity, Falshood, Evasion, Inconsistency, Innovation, Imposition, Infidelity, Hypocrisy, Pride, Raillery, Apostacy, Perjury, Idolatry, Villany, Blasphemy, Abomination, Confusion, and Worse than Turkish Tyranny. Most justly exhibited, and offered to be proved against the most noted Leaders, etc. of the People called Quakers.* London, 1716.

4. Opposition and Controversial Works Not Yet Located

Dunton, John. *Stinking Fish: Or, A Foolish Poem.* To be published in a second part, scheduled for December 1708: "19. The False Prophet, or Bunhill Fool." This was probably never printed.

Lions, Jean. *Caractere des six ministres de la Savoye.* Possibly not by Lions.

———. *Examen de la prétendue réfutation de l'apologie de Jean Lions.*

The New Prophets Proved to be Divine.

New Prophets: their historical and true picture. Broadside engraving, folio, 1708. Depicts the prophets at the council table, in six smaller scenes.

ODE à la gloire immortelle de l'incomparable Mr. Max. M[isson].

Owen, Charles. *The Scene of Delusions . . . historical account of prophetick impostures.* London(?), 1712.

The Prophets Catechism.

Relation apologétique de la conduite du consistoire de la Savoye.

Relation touchant M. Lions.

Réponse à la relation de Lions.

[Rival, Pierre]. *Reponse au declaration de M. Jean Lions.*

———. *Suite de la réponse au declaration.*

5. Newspapers and Journals Cited

British Apollo. Or, Curious Amusements for the Ingenious (1708).

Censura Temporum: The Good or Ill Tendencies of Books, Sermons, Pamphlets, etc. Impartially considered. In a Dialogue between Eubulus and Sophronius (1708–10).

Defoe, Daniel, ed. *Review of the State of the English Nation* (1707–9).

English Post (1707–9).

History of the Works of the Learned. Or, An Impartial Account of Books Lately Printed in all Parts of Europe (1707–10).

Humours of a Coffee-House: A Comedy As it is Dayly Acted (1707). Continued as *The Weekly Comedy* (1707).

Nouvelles de la république des lettres (Amsterdam), June, July, September 1707, January, February, April 1708. This journal included articles by English correspondents.

The Observator (1707–8).

Post-Boy (1706–9).

Rehearsal of the Observator [*Or, A View of the Times*] (1707–9).

The Spectator (1711).

6. Medicine and Enthusiasm

Addison, Joseph. *Spectator* 201 (October 20, 1711).

Allen, Benjamin. *The Natural History of the Chalybeat and Purging Waters of England, With their particular Essays and Uses.* London, 1699.

Brydall, John. *Non compos mentis; or the Law relating to Natural fools, Madfolks, and Lunatick Persons, Inquisited, and Explained, for Common Benefit.* London, 1700.

Casaubon, Meric. *A Treatise concerning Enthusiasme, As it is an Effect of Nature: but is mistaken by many for either Divine Inspiration, or Diabolical Possession.* London, 1655.

Cheyne, George. *The English Malady; or a Treatise of Nervous Diseases of all Kinds.* London, 1733.

Cooper, Anthony Ashley, third earl of Shaftesbury. *A Letter concerning Enthusiasm, to My Lord *****.* London, 1708.

————. *Several Letters written by a Noble Lord to a Young Man at the University.* London, 1716.

Fallowes, Thomas. *The Best Method for the Cure of Lunatics. With some Account of the Incomparable Oleum Cephalicum Used in the same, Prepared and Administered.* London, 1705.

[Fowler, Edward]. *Reflections Upon a Letter concerning Enthusiasm To my Lord *****. In another Letter to a Lord.* London, 1709.

[Harris, John]. *A Letter to the Fatal Triumvirate: In Answer to That pretended to be written by Dr. Byfield.* London, 1719.

Harvey, Gideon. *Morbus anglicus, or a Theoretick and Practical Discourse of Consumptions, and Hypochondriack Melancholy.* London, 1666. Copy at Yale University.

Harvey, James. *Praesagium Medicum, Or, the Prognostick Signs of Acute Diseases.* London, 1706.

Irish, David. *Levamen infirmi: or, cordial counsel to the sick and diseased.* London, 1700. Copy at the Library of the New York Academy of Medicine, New York City.

Locke, John. *An Essay Concerning Human Understanding.* Edited by A.C. Fraser. 2 vols. New York, 1959 [1690, 4th ed. 1700].

Mandeville, Bernard de. *A Treatise of the Hypochondriack and Hysterick Passions, Vulgarly called the Hypo in Men, and Vapours in Women.* London, 1711.

More, Henry. *Enthusiasmus Triumphatus; Or, a Brief Discourse of The Nature, Causes, Kinds, and Cure of Enthusiasm.* London, 1656. Included in *A Collection of Several Philosophical Writings of Henry More.* London, 1662.

Nicholson, Henry. *A Brief Treatise of the Anatomy of Humane Bodies. . . . Demonstrating the Circulation of the Blood, and all Muscular Motion from the Pressure of the Atmosphere.* London, 1709.

Purcell, John. *A Treatise of Vapours, or Hysterick Fits.* London, 1707.

Remarks on the Letter to a Lord concerning Enthusiasm. In a Letter to a Gentleman. Not written in Raillery, Yet in Good Humour. London, 1708.

Salmon, William. *Iatrica: Seu Praxis Medendi. The Practice of Curing Diseases. . . . To which is newly added, as an Appendix, Observations upon the Lethargy, Carus, Frenzy, Madness, Defects of the Internal Senses, and Hurts of the External Senses.* London, 1694. Copy at Yale University.

Swift, Jonathan. *A Discourse concerning the Mechanical Operation of the Spirit. In a Letter to a Friend. A Fragment.* London, 1704. Bound and paged consecutively with his *A Tale of a Tub*, 2d ed., corrected. London, 1704.

Sydenham, Humphrey. *Dr. Sydenham's Compleat Method of Curing Almost All Diseases, and Description of their Symptoms. To which are now Added, Five Discourses of the same Author concerning the Pleurisy, Gout, Hysterical Passion, Dropsy and Rheumatism. Abridged, and faithfully Translated out of the Original Latin.* 3d ed. London, 1697.

Willis, Thomas. *The London Practice of Physick: Or the whole Practical Part of Physick Contained in the Works of Dr. Willis.* London, 1685.

Wotton, William [Mary Astell]. *Bart'lemy Fair; or, An Enquiry after Wit: In which due Respect is had to a Letter concerning Enthusiasm, To my Lord *****.* London, 1709.

Index

Index

UNIVERSITY OF FLORIDA MONOGRAPHS

Social Sciences

1. *The Whigs of Florida, 1845–1854*, by Herbert J. Doherty, Jr.
2. *Austrian Catholics and the Social Question, 1918–1933*, by Alfred Diamant
3. *The Siege of St. Augustine in 1702*, by Charles W. Arnade
4. *New Light on Early and Medieval Japanese Historiography*, by John A. Harrison
5. *The Swiss Press and Foreign Affairs in World War II*, by Frederick H. Hartmann
6. *The American Militia: Decade of Decision, 1789–1800*, by John K. Mahon
7. *The Foundation of Jacques Maritain's Political Philosophy*, by Hwa Yol Jung
8. *Latin American Population Studies*, by T. Lynn Smith
9. *Jacksonian Democracy on the Florida Frontier*, by Arthur W. Thompson
10. *Holman Versus Hughes: Extension of Australian Commonwealth Powers*, by Conrad Joyner
11. *Welfare Economics and Subsidy Programs*, by Milton Z. Kafoglis
12. *Tribune of the Slavophiles: Konstantin Aksokov*, by Edward Chmielewski
13. *City Managers in Politics: An Analysis of Manager Tenure and Termination*, by Gladys M. Kammerer,

Charles D. Farris, John M. DeGrove, and Alfred B. Clubok
14. *Recent Southern Economic Development as Revealed by the Changing Structure of Employment*, by Edgar S. Dunn, Jr.
15. *Sea Power and Chilean Independence*, by Donald E. Worcester
16. *The Sherman Antitrust Act and Foreign Trade*, by Andre Simmons
17. *The Origins of Hamilton's Fiscal Policies*, by Donald F. Swanson
18. *Criminal Asylum in Anglo-Saxon Law*, by Charles H. Riggs, Jr.
19. *Colonia Barón Hirsch, A Jewish Agricultural Colony in Argentina*, by Morton D. Winsberg
20. *Time Deposits in Present-Day Commercial Banking*, by Lawrence L. Crum
21. *The Eastern Greenland Case in Historical Perspective*, by Oscar Svarlien
22. *Jacksonian Democracy and the Historians*, by Alfred A. Cave
23. *The Rise of the American Chemistry Profession, 1850–1900*, by Edward H. Beardsley
24. *Aymara Communities and the Bolivian Agrarian Reform*, by William E. Carter
25. *Conservatives in the Progressive*